LeanSpeak

The Productivity Business Improvement Dictionary

LeanSpeak

The Productivity Business Improvement Dictionary

Compiled and edited by Mary A. Junewick
from materials owned by
Productivity Press and The Productivity Group

Productivity Press • Portland, Oregon

Additional copies of this book are available from the publisher. Discounts are available for multiple copies through the Sales Department (800-394-6868). Address all other inquiries to:

Productivity Press
P.O. Box 13390
Portland, Oregon 97213-0390
United States of America
Telephone: 503-235-0600
Telefax: 503-235-0909
Email: info@productivityinc.com

Cover design by Stephen Scates
Page design by Lorraine Millard
Page composition by William H. Brunson Typography Services
Printed and bound by Malloy Lithographing, Inc. in the United States of America

Library of Congress Cataloging-in-Publication Data
    Leanspeak : the productivity business improvement dictionary / compiled and edited by Mary A. Junewick from materials owned by Productivity Press and the Productivity Group
       p. cm.
    Includes bibliographical references.
    ISBN 1-56327-275-X
    1. Industrial management–Dictionaries.   2. Industrial productivity—Dictionaries.   I. Junewick, Mary A.

HD30.15 .L423   2002
650'.03—dc21

2002001211

06 05 04 03 02   6 5 4 3 2 1

Publisher's Message

For more than twenty years, Productivity has been teaching the elements of lean management and lean production. Our consultants, trainers, and publications have helped thousands of companies in the United States and around the world learn how to implement lean methods. We, in turn, have learned from their experiences.

Over these years, a large vocabulary of lean concepts and strategies has evolved. As different companies have modified these concepts and strategies to fit their own circumstances and needs, some confusion and misunderstanding has occurred. Productivity Press has compiled the *LeanSpeak* dictionary with two objectives in mind: to end some of the confusion and to help you become knowledgeable and comfortable in conversations about lean. The information in *LeanSpeak* has been drawn from the large collection of Productivity Press publications and Productivity Group training materials. We are pleased to share this compendium of lean knowledge with you.

This is the first printed version of *LeanSpeak*, which was originally released as an ebook. We have expanded a few definitions and added some new entries. We will continue to add entries, as well as refine and expand current definitions in future printings. We invite and welcome your comments, criticisms, and suggestions — so that we can make this the most complete and helpful lean dictionary available. Write to us at leanspeak@productivityinc.com.

Within Productivity, thanks go to Judith Allen, Vice President of Product Development, for her support and encouragement of the project; to Mary A. Junewick for project management, content development, and copy-editing; to Toni Chiapelli for proofreading; to Stephen Scates for cover design; to Lorraine Millard for electronic page design and composition (also for technical research and advice on the original ebook); and to Michael Ryder for the *LeanSpeak* title and print management.

A special thank you to Tom Jackson, CEO of Productivity, for his expert comments and suggestions. It is his hope that this dictionary will one day be expanded and refined into a comprehensive encyclopedia of lean. Thanks also to Productivity Group trainers and consultants Richard Niedermeier, Charles Skinner, and Paul McGrath for their expert content review.

Thanks to Productivity Press members Don Wills for a dictionary review (and for web research and management on the original ebook); to Ed Hanus for sales and marketing guidance, as well as a dictionary review; and to Lydia Junewick, Bettina Katz, and Jeff Myers for their marketing and promotion efforts.

Two lean business leaders were most kind to "guest review" our dictionary and give helpful feedback. Thank you to Ray Keefe, Vice President of Manufacturing of Emerson Electric; and John Davis, formerly plant manager and corporate trainer for United Technologies, now consultant and author of *Fast Track to Waste-Free Manufacturing* and *Leading the Lean Initiative*, available from Productivity Press.

Sean Jones
Publisher

Note: words that are shown in bold in the text of an entry are cross-references to other entries you may find useful in understanding or expanding upon the definition.

5S: See **five S**.

80/20 rule: See **Pareto principle**.

A

ABC: See **activity-based costing**.

ABM: See **activity-based management**.

abnormality: any process or equipment condition that does not conform to the standard conditions required for the scheduled production and delivery of quality products and services.

accelerated testing: testing by creating upper-limit conditions to shorten the time in which failure might occur. For example, running electronic components in higher than normal temperature environments to test their reliability. The result of this engineering test is obtained by dividing the acceleration test factor time (A1) into the expected norm usage time.

accept quality level (AQL): a rating of the maximum proportion of defective units that can be considered a tolerable average out of a sample. The ideal level is, of course, **zero defects**.

accumulators: a collection of **kanban** signals at the supplying work center that operate until a specified level of demand has been attained. These logistical accumulators help in mitigating setups, producing higher mixes, prioritizing, preventing buffer depletion, and managing the supply to several consumers. The more traditional use of the term refers to physical accumulators, collection devices used in large expanses on an automated line where product is stacked or racked between operations.

accuracy: the congruence between any observed value and its reference value. Contrast with **bias**.

action-items flip chart: a "to-do" flip chart that can be used in the work cell as a daily updated visual display of cell activities—who will take action, when, where, why, and how.

actions: as responses to a manufacturing problem, actions can be differentiated in this way: *Adaptive actions* are those taken immediately to respond to the problem before thoroughly investigating the **root cause**. Adaptive action allows you to live with the problem while minimizing additional damage from it. *Mitigating actions* are those taken to reduce the severity of the problem. *Corrective actions* are the countermeasures you take against root or contributing causes of the problem. *Monitoring actions* are performed to check the effectiveness of your corrective actions. Sometimes monitoring actions will uncover further problems that must be fixed.

activity: all those things that people in organizations do that result in the work flow of products and services being produced and delivered to customers.

activity-based costing (ABC): a highly accurate management accounting system that assigns cost to products based on the actual amount of work required to produce them. "Work" includes various resources and activities (floor space, raw materials, machine hours, and human effort). Contrast with **target costing** and **standard costing**.

activity-based management (ABM): a common sense, systematic method of planning, controlling, and improving labor and overhead cost. Activity-based management portrays a business as a series of activities related to customer requirements, each of which have an average cost attached to them. By measuring activities rather than traditional departmental costs, a business can focus on cross-functional processes to identify non value-adding activities and pinpoint the true drivers of cost at each stage. The basic building block for activity-based management is *activity accounting*, which defines and reports the activities, costs, activity characteristics, and outputs of each department, cost center, or group of employees in an organization (also known as *activity-based accounting*).

activity board: an information board prepared by an improvement group to facilitate communication and understanding between operators or group members and used to display the performance and status of the group to other frontline personnel.

address: an easy-to-read label affixed to a particular place to identify that place for people working in a factory or office. A **return-address** is a corresponding label affixed to an object such as a tool or package of material indicating where it should be returned or stored. Addresses and return-addresses reduce non-value-adding search time. They can be used in **five S** and **visual control systems**. On a **kanban card**, the address is the section of the card specifying the location of the material when staged and its destination when consumed.

affinity diagram: a visual display of a team's brainstorming and consensus activities that sorts and summarizes large amounts of information (ideas, issues, opinions) into relevant groupings. See **business process tools** for links to other tools.

agile manufacturing: a manufacturing approach with techniques designed to contribute to the flexibility of a process and thereby reduce the impact of changes in product mix and, to a certain extent, volume.

alignment: occurs when two or more people have their sights set on the same goals and objectives and share common beliefs about the best ways of achieving them. In a lean organization, alignment is achieved through the process of **policy management**.

allowable cost: the allowed manufacturing cost determined by finding the difference between the target selling price and the target profit margin. See **cost** for links to a variety of cost definitions.

andon: a device that calls attention to defects, equipment abnormalities, and other problems, or reports the status and needs of a system by means of *lights*. There are three-color and four-color andons. From top to bottom, the three-color andon has a red light for failure mode, an amber light to show marginal performance, and a green light for normal operation mode. Four-color andons add the color blue (lack of material to run) in third position and push green to the bottom of the andon array. Andons are attached to a specific machine or machining center and represent the condition of *that* machine or machining center. The term "andon" is often used incorrectly to apply to any signals or combinations thereof, such as lights and audible alarms. Audible alarms are part of a robust signaling system and may accompany andon signals but they are not andons. See also **annunciator board** and **visual control**.

annunciator board: a multi-station board over an assembly line to report on the condition of several grouped but physically disconnected operations in a single process stream. There are different colored lights in each square indicating the condition of each station on the line that the board is representing. Each of the squares is represented by a corresponding **andon** at each station. Also called a *line board*.

Apollonian management: a management style based on data gathering, careful measurement, attention to details, analysis of facts, reason, sober judgment, and prudent evaluation of costs and benefits. This approach is valuable for information gathering, measurement, and problem-solving in the lean organization. Contrast with **Dionysian** and **Promethean** management.

AQL: See **accept quality level**.

area map and arrow diagram: a representation of equipment, parts storage, people, etc. in the workplace, with the direction of material movement depicted by arrows. Used to improve workplace layout, processes, and work flow.

as-if cost: the projected cost of a future product if it were manufactured today, taking into consideration all the cost-reduction opportunities that were identified when the previous generation of products was being designed and manufactured. See **cost** for links to variety of cost definitions.

assembly process analysis chart: a chart used to show the sequence of operations performed on an assembly line and to whom these jobs are assigned.

asset management: the systematic planning and control of a physical resource throughout its economic life.

audit: the systematic examination of activities, policies, procedures, and instructions as to their implementation, performance, results, and records. There are numerous perspectives from which to describe audits. Compliance and gap audits scrutinize a company's quality system. A company may perform an internal audit (by the company on itself) or external audits (by the company on its suppliers). Extrinsic audits are performed on the company by a regulatory body or inspection agency. Audits can examine products or systems. An attribute audit is one where questions are answered with a yes or no without other score or scaled evaluation. Such audits are pass or fail in nature.

authoritarian management: traditional *command-and-control* or *chain-of-command* approach to quality, productivity, cost management, and all other aspects of business. In this system decisions are made by the leadership and are passed down through the organization with little or no intermediate control or decision making. Directives are to be followed without question.

auto-inserter: a device that automatically inserts work pieces into a machine for processing or assembly. Auto inserters also insert parts into products.

automated inventory replenishment: a supply chain supplier/buyer agreement in which the supplier maintains the inventories of its parts at the buyer's site by responding to the buyer's automatic refill orders.

automation with a human touch: See **autonomation**.

autonomation: the second of the two major pillars of the Toyota Production system (the first being **just-in-time**), autonomation is the transfer of human intelligence to automated machinery so that machines are able to stop, start, load, and unload automatically, as well as detect the production of a defective part, stop themselves, and signal for help. It frees operators for other value-added work. This concept has also been known as *automation with a human touch* and *jidoka*. Sakichi Toyoda pioneered this concept at the turn of the twentieth century when he invented automatic looms that stopped instantly when any thread broke. This enabled one operator to manage many machines without risk of producing vast amounts of defective cloth. Compare to **mistake-proofing**.

autonomous maintenance: a component of **total productive maintenance** that involves production machine operators in step-by-step activities to ensure optimum conditions of machine operation. The steps of autonomous maintenance include initial cleaning and inspection, eliminating contamination and inaccessible parts, establishing provisional standards for regular equipment care, skills training in equipment subsystems, conducting general inspections, and managing and controlling the work process and environment. It achieves the transfer of basic, unskilled maintenance activities to *nonmaintenance personnel*—the machine operators.

availability: the period of scheduled time for which an asset is capable of performing its specified function—expressed as a percentage.

availability loss: also referred to as *downtime loss*, this loss occurs due to equipment failures and setup time. (In some factories, loss due to replacing broken cutting tools, loss of productivity at startup, and time outs for meetings, breaks, etc., are also counted as availability/downtime losses.) Contrast with **performance loss** and **quality loss**. See also **six big losses**.

B

B2B: See **business to business**.

backflush: a technique, usually computer-based, whereby individually purchased parts, subassemblies, assemblies, and major modules, are not transacted in the inventory control system until the finished product or major assembly stage is completed. At this completion point, all applicable inventory/labor adjustments are made at the same time.

baka-yoke: a Japanese term that literally means "fool-proofing." Abandoned by Shigeo Shingo in favor of the term **poka-yoke**, or "innocent mistake-proofing," to avoid the personal criticism implied by the term baka-yoke. See **mistake-proofing**.

balanced scorecard: a measurement system that enables a company to clarify its vision and strategy and translate them into action. The scorecard balances identified metrics against the intent of the current plan and gives weight to those that are more important. It helps a company weigh financial and nonfinancial impacts and establish lean performance measurables. Key areas often assessed in the balanced scorecard are customer relations, financial management, internal business processes, employee performance, and organizational learning and innovation.

Baldrige award: See **Malcolm Baldrige National Quality Award**.

bar code: the sequence of vertical bars and spaces that can be read by a light sensitive laser beam and translated into digital data used by a computer. The bar code can represent numbers and/or other symbols and is affixed to an item to identify it by product number, cost, location, etc.

Manufacturers use bar codes to track the movement of parts through manufacturing, warehousing, and shipping. There are several different systems currently in use in industry and bar codes are unique to each system. The bar code will almost always include the stock-keeping unit (SKU) number for an item, subassembly, or salable unit, which makes bar code scanning a very sophisticated way of keeping track of SKU inventory levels. Compare to **stock-keeping unit**.

barony: a supply chain network with multiple **core firms**. Each core firm is referred to as a *baron*. Contrast with **kingdom**. See also **republic**.

baseline measure: a statistic or numerical value for the current performance level of a process or function. Typical performance measurements requiring a baseline measure are on-time delivery, dock to dock, inventory turns, etc. A baseline needs to be taken before improvement activities are begun to accurately reflect the rate of improvement or new level of attainment of the performance being measured. Setting performance baselines is an essential early step to attaining the lean enterprise.

batch-and-queue: refers to the usual movement of part lots in mass-production practices. Typically, large lots of a part are made and sent as a batch to wait in queue for the next operation in the production process. Contrast with **one-piece flow**.

bathtub curve: a measurement curve that describes the failure rate of a system or a device as it is goes through its life cycle. The initial, random, and wear-out failure periods give the curve its bathtub shape. When the curve slopes downward (the initial failure period) the failure rate is decreasing with usage. Here is where manufacturing problems are typically encountered and corrected (or the system fails). This curve can be shortened by **early equipment management**. Failure rate is constant during the flat (random failure) part of the curve. **Preventive maintenance** and **focused equipment improvement** can minimize failures. On the upward slope (the wear-out failure period), the failure rate is increasing with usage and the system or device is approaching the end of its life cycle. This curve can be deferred through **autonomous maintenance** activities.

benchmark: a qualitative and/or quantitative performance measure of an activity or activities enacted at one or more enterprises that are considered best in class. A benchmark helps a company set goals in the strategic or tactical phase of an implementation. The comparison is usually made between companies competing for the same market shares but can also be done on the basis of a single similar function even if the enterprises are from different industries and participate in different markets.

benchmark allowable cost: the allowable cost of a product if it was designed and manufactured by the most efficient manufacturer in the industry. See **cost** for links to a variety of cost definitions.

best estimate: in this estimate, there is a 50 percent chance that a true reading will be higher or lower than what is anticipated.

best practices: methods that have been established in the industry as effectively improving the workplace and which can be passed on from one area of a business to another or from one business to another. As levels of performance improve, best practices will naturally evolve.

bias: the difference or distortion between the average observed value and a reference value. Contrast with **accuracy**.

bill of materials (BOM): the list of all the subassemblies, parts, and raw materials that go into a parent assembly, usually structured in hierarchical layers form gross assemblies to minor items.

black belt: a *full-time* team leader who has passed an *advanced level* of training in six-sigma improvement methodology. The black belt is responsible for implementing process or quality improvement projects within his or her company. Graduates of this four-phase six sigma training are considered masters in measurement, analysis, process improvement, and process control. See **green belt** and **master black belt**.

BOM: See **bill of materials**.

bottleneck: the place in a production line that adversely affects throughput. See **constraint**. As a resource capacity limitation, a bottleneck will not allow a system to meet the demand of the customer.

boundaryless organization: Jack Welch's term for organizations without functional **silos**. See **cross-functional management**.

BPR: See **business process reengineering**.

brainstorming: a method of unlocking creativity and generating ideas that is very effective for teams. In the first step, ideas are offered without the constraints of critical evaluation or judgment. The idea is to "let go." After any and all ideas have been listened to, no matter how "far-fetched," the ideas are then critically evaluated to select the best ones. See **business process tools** for links to other tools.

breakdowns: partial or complete loss of equipment function. Breakdowns are more time-consuming and costly than temporary **minor stoppages**. **Total productive maintenance** is the overarching system used to prevent **equipment breakdowns** and reap maximum use of machines.

breakthrough engineering: Finding the technological, process, or knowledge breakthroughs to solve design bottlenecks and improve the product or service. Also called *bottleneck* engineering.

breakthrough strategies: imaginative, trail-breaking moves that set activities going in a direction that permits escape from previous conceptual or physical constraints.

brownfield: a design or production facility that has been operating for some time with traditional **mass-production** methods and entrenched systems of social organization. Contrast with **greenfield**.

BTS: See **build to schedule**.

buffer stock: finished goods available within the value steam to meet takt time due to variations *in customer demand*. Also called *buffer inventory*. Contrast with **safety stock**. The reduction of buffer and safety stock is always a target of continuous improvement.

build to schedule (BTS): the measure that tells how well a plant produces the correct volume, mix, and sequence according to what the customer wants. First the volume, mix, and sequence performances are calculated. The build-to-schedule rate then = volume x mix x sequence. (To calculate **volume**, divide the actual number of units produced by the number of units that were scheduled [ordered]. To calculate **mix**, divide the actual units built to mix by the actual units produced or scheduled [whichever is less]. To calculate **sequence**, divide the actual units built to sequence by the actual units built to mix.) See **manufacturing measurables** for links to other measurables.

business process tools: a large variety of tools to help an organization become lean. A few of the more common tools are described in this dictionary. See **affinity diagram, brainstorming, CEDAC, control chart, cost of quality, decision tree, fault-tree analysis, focus group, force-field analysis, gap analysis, histogram, house of quality, Johari's window, matrix diagram, Pareto chart, process mapping, quality chart/table, run chart, scatter diagram, value analysis, variance analysis,** and **window analysis**.

For a thorough compilation of tools, including instructions on how to use them, see Walter Michalski's *Tool Navigator: The Master Guide for Teams* (Productivity Press). There you will find tools to help with various process categories such as team building, data collecting, analyzing/trending, idea generating, decision-making, evaluating/selecting, changing/implementing, and planning/presenting.

business process reengineering (BPR): the radical redesign of business processes based on rethinking what the ideal or theoretically perfect design would be and then building it. Business process reengineering uses a combination of value stream mapping, value analysis, and technology enablers to reduce cost through reduced lead times and headcount. See **value stream mapping** and **value analysis**. The BPR movement has been largely a failure because organizations often did not address the cultural issues of strategic change. The movement is still relevant because BPR methods will become useful as lean organizations move into the final phases of implementation, where all business processes—not just manufacturing processes—must be transformed.

business renewal: a strategically initiated process of periodically reevaluating all of the enterprise's organizational functions to redefine its strengths, core capabilities, competencies, business direction, improvement opportunities, market focus, etc. The outcome of this process is a strategic plan that will define direction and measurements for the long and/or short term.

business to business (B2B): online transactions between one business, institution, or government agency and another as contrasted to transactions from a business to a consumer (B2C).

C

CAD: See **computer-aided design**.

CAM: See **computer-aided manufacturing**.

capacity planning: the process of predicting if and
when system saturation will occur. This includes
determining maximum user load and throughput,
how the work load will evolve, and what the desired
performance levels will be. *Capacity management*
involves planning enhancements to the current system and evaluating the design of new systems.

catalyst: anyone in the lean organization who does not
tell and instruct, but who, with discussion and dia-
logue, challenges others to think, plan, and work
more effectively.

catchball: often referred to as *hoshin kanri* (policy
management), this give-and-take activity is performed between different levels of the organization
to make sure that critical information on goals and
objectives as well as feedback is passed back and
forth. Catchball is actually a discrete phase of the
policy management process in which leaders
deploy strategies and budgets to managers throughout the organization, and managers confirm that
they understand the leadership's expectations by
re-interpreting strategies and budgets and feeding
back their understanding—often with suggestions
for changes—to the leaders. Catchball ensures
that all levels are aligned in direction, strategy,

implementation, assessment, measurement, and resources. An integral part of the business renewal process, it ensures that targets set at a higher level are passed down to the next level to ascertain their feasibility.

causal-loop analysis: a system dynamics tool used to describe and diagram a situation in terms of perspective, time frame, problem behaviors, and policies (choices). It is used to better understand and respond to problem behaviors.

cause: the reason or factor contributing to an effect or "problem." Any attempt to solve a manufacturing problem will uncover more than one kind of cause. The *root cause* is the most basic reason for the problem. If the root cause is corrected, the problem will not recur. A *contributing* cause is a condition that could not have caused the problem by itself but which needs to be recognized and corrected to improve the process or product. A *potential cause* is a condition that looks as if it *may* have caused the problem but the connection between it and the problem needs to be verified. A *presumptive cause* emerges from data collected at the beginning of, or during, an investigation. It is a *hypothetical cause* that seems *logically* to have been able to cause the problem, but it needs to be validated. See **common cause** and **special cause**. See also **root cause**.

cause-and-effect diagram with the addition of cards (CEDAC): a continuous improvement technique that uses a wall chart and **color-coded cards** to enable workers to set goals, identify problems and causes, and gather ideas for responding to and solving them. Further steps generated by the CEDAC process include testing ideas, adopting them, standardizing them, and deploying their adherence. CEDAC is an enhancement to the widely used Ishikawa "fishbone" diagramming for problem solving because it is iterative and dynamic. Dr. Ryuji Fukuda initiated this evolutionary step and was awarded the Deming Prize for it. The method is best used for team-based problem solving to analyze the characteristics of a process or situation. Dr. Fukuda later expanded this technique into a comprehensive strategic improvement process—see **system for enhancing daily activities through creativity (SEDAC)**. See also **business process tools** for links to other tools.

CEDAC: See **cause-and-effect diagram with the addition of cards**.

cell: a logical, efficient, and usually physically self-contained arrangement of machinery, tooling, and personnel to complete a production sequence. The cell enables **one-piece flow** and **multi-process handling**. Each cell has a leader who manages the workflow and is responsible for maintaining quality and productivity. Also called a *work cell*. Contrast with **process village**. See also **cell layout**.

cell design: the technique of creating and improving cells to optimize their one-piece flow. A quality cell design will result in improved space utilization, higher value-adding ratios, shorter lead times, lower work-in-process inventories, simplified production of part families, and optimal use of employees. See **process design analysis sheet**.

cell layout: the arrangement of the cell. Some principles of good layout include arranging the work sequentially, using a counter clockwise flow, putting machines close together (but not too close for safety and maintenance activity), putting the last operation close to the first (typically, but not always, in a "U" or "C" shape), and homogenous production. See **U-shaped cell**.

cellular manufacturing: manufacturing by the use of cells. See **cell**.

chained target costing: occurs when the buyer's **target costing** system provides the target selling prices for the supplier's target costing system. See also **target costing chain**.

chaku-chaku: Japanese term meaning "load-load." It is the method in **one-piece flow** in which the operator proceeds from machine to machine, taking a part from the previous machine and loading the part into the next machine.

champion: an individual, from any level of the organization, who has the authority and responsibility to inform, support, and direct a team effort to implement and integrate a new tool, method, technique, or technology, etc. The champion is a first-line resource for all the participants and, in some cases, has the authority to allocate the organization's resources during the life of the project. Also called *lean champion* or *project champion*.

In six sigma programs, the term is used to refer to two different kinds of executive-level six sigma sponsors. Deployment champions are responsible for implementing and nurturing six sigma throughout the organization. Project champions function at the business-unit level to oversee **black belts** and handle project-specific concerns.

change agent: an individual who acts as a catalyst for organizational change.

changeover: the *physical components* of the changeover process might involve the installation of a new tool in a metalworking machine, different paint in a painting system, new plastic resin and mold in an injection molding machine, or new software in a computer, etc., needed whenever a production device is assigned to perform a different operation. As Shigeo Shingo wanted us to understand, however, successful changeover involves more than just these physical changes. It includes the total time it takes to prepare a resource to once again *add value* to the value stream. See **changeover time**.

Physical changeover includes managing both internal and external changeover activities. *Internal* activities are those that must be performed while the machine is shut down or idle (adjusting, removing, replacing dies, tools, fixtures, guides, etc.). *External* activities are those that can be performed while the machine is running or producing (getting stock or tools, cleaning the area, paperwork). See **simultaneous** and **successive changeover**.

changeover time: the time between the last good piece off one production run and the first good piece off the next run, amplified by specific equipment or process requirements.

changeover waste: the waste of machine downtime while a production line is modified to produce a different product.

charter: a document (sometimes poster size) that clearly defines the mission, scope, activities, participants, time line, risks, and deliverables for an improvement effort. A *team charter* identifies these parameters for a team such as a focused **kaizen** team.

chronic loss: the gap between actual equipment effectiveness and its optimal potential when a loss recurs *within a usual range*. Chronic losses are complex and hard to solve. There can be multiple causes and hidden abnormalities. A key to solving chronic loss is innovation, but chronic losses are often accepted and problem solving is neglected. Contrast with **sporadic loss**. See **statistical process control**.

CMMS: See **computerized maintenance management software/system**.

CNC machine: See **computer numerical control machine**.

coach: a team builder, mentor, and role model for lean improvement groups within the organization.

color-coded cards: teams using CEDAC and mistake-proofing charts or other CEDAC-based problem-solving methods use these cards to collect and display information. Categories, problems, and improvement targets are written on *pink cards*. *Yellow cards* are used to identify all the facts (causes) getting in the way of the target(s). Ideas for solving the various problems are written on *blue cards*. After all the perspectives have been collected and organized, the idea cards are evaluated and tested. Because the cards are movable, they can be easily regrouped, and charts can be re-used for the next team effort.

co-makership: a strategically driven initiative that focuses on *joining with suppliers of goods and services* to include them in the process of defining and delivering value to the organization. Two implementation techniques are quality function deployment and CEDAC. Compare to **strategic partnering**.

common cause: a cause that is *chronic*, usual, and due to chance factors (natural variation). Contrast with **special cause**. See **control chart** and **statistical process control** for further discussion.

companywide quality management (CQM): an initiative that has grown out of **total quality management** to enlist *all* personnel in maximizing the quality of *all* operations and processes in the company.

compliance: an indication or judgment or state in which an activity, product, service, or document meets the specifications or regulations set for it.

computer-aided design (CAD): using a computer instead of hand drawings to design things—from small items to airplanes and buildings. With CAD, an engineer can look at a design from different angles and zoom in or out for close-up or long-distance views. Also, the program keeps track of design dependencies, so that when an engineer changes one value, all other dependent values are automatically changed. there are a variety of CAD software programs.

computer-aided manufacturing (CAM): a system that uses a computer to design *and* manufacture products. With CAM, an engineer can not only control the design of a product but the manufactruring processes used to create it. For example, once a product has been designed with a CAM component, the design itself will exert control on the machines that produce the parts. Three types of CAM systems used to automate a factory are real-time control, **robotics**, and **materials requirements planning** systems. All are concerned with automatically directing the manufacture and inventory of parts. See **computer-aided design**.

computer numerical control (CNC) machine: a versatile and sophisticated machine used in manufacturing for its complex motion control capabilities, which offer improved automation, consistent and accurate work pieces, and flexibility. Two popular types of CNC machine applications are found in machining and turning centers.

computerized maintenance management software/system (CMMS): a software system that interfaces with company logistics and helps with the management of assets, work orders, purchasing, inventory control, preventive maintenance, and other maintenance. There are a variety of these systems.

concurrent cost management: occurs when two firms coordinate their cost management programs to contain costs early on. For example, a buyer and supplier may begin working together in the design phase when the buyer outsources the research and development of a major function to the supplier.

concurrent engineering: a cross-organizational, cross-functional team effort to manage a new product from its conception all the way through to the achievement of its targeted cost and profit. Product functionality and quality is enhanced at both at the supplier output level and the end product level. Also called *lean engineering* and *simultaneous engineering*.

conformance: often used as a synonym for **compliance,** it more properly applies to characteristics of objects than to activities or documents.

consensus: an agreement to agree between two or more persons. After having had the opportunity to express an opinion and influence the final decision, each member of a decision-making group agrees to support the final decision, even though any one or more members may not be in complete accord with all the particulars of the decision.

constituents: See **stakeholders**.

constraint: an operation included in a specific process sequence—operational or administrative—that has the lowest output rate when compared to the balance of the other operations in the process. There is normally only one constraint at a time in a process sequence but there is almost always at least one. The constraint prevents an enterprise from serving its customers better and making more money. There are typically four types of constraints: physical (a bottleneck), logistical (for example, response time), managerial (policies and rules), and behavioral (the activities of a particular employee or group of employees). See **bottleneck**. See also **theory of constraints**.

continuous flow: See **one-piece flow**.

continuous improvement: this means improvement in *small, incremental, continuous,* steps that can be placed in the context of a number of tactical initiatives. Daily improvement in small amounts carried out in every job and function of the business eventually accumulates into very large gains. The term is a loose translation of the Japanese **gemba kaizen** (shopfloor improvement) and is sometimes used incorrectly to refer to *any* change initiative, particularly sudden and dramatic change (**kaikaku**).

control board: a visual display of performance-related information for the workplace, updated in real time by the area work team whose performance is being displayed. This visual control/visual management technique communicates current production levels, takt time, safety, training plan, etc. Also called a *performance analysis* or *performance measures board.*

control chart: a graph that plots randomly selected data points over time to determine if a process is performing to requirements or is under statistical control. The control chart shows whether a problem is caused by an unusual or special cause or (and is correctable) or is due to common chance causes alone (natural variation). It focuses on a single part attribute, process parameter, or standardized activity. See **chronic loss, sporadic loss,** and **statistical process control**. See **business process tools** for links to other tools.

control part: the critical part of an end product that goes through all core manufacturing processes from beginning to end. The control part is used to help calculate various other manufacturing measurables. See **manufacturing measurables** for links to other measurables.

core competency: an internal capability central to or critical to the success of the business, which, if taken away, would drastically change the direction of the business and the products or services delivered to clients. For example, an accounting firm might have auditing, business evaluation, financial reporting, and human resources as capabilities. If their human resources activities were outsourced, it would hardly affect their business direction or services. If auditing were outsourced, however, it would significantly impact the business because it is one of their core competencies.

core firm: a firm in a supplier network that has a power advantage because its goods and services are disproportionately sought after in the network. See **barony**.

core team: the group primarily responsible for completing a designated part of a lean manufacturing plan. Also called *core implementation team*.

corrective action: action carried out to correct a non-compliance. See **compliance**.

corrective maintenance: modifying existing equipment to improve performance or adapting new equipment to meet changing manufacturing needs.

cost: a number of different methods are used to estimate or determine the "cost" of manufacturing a product. See **allowable cost, as-if cost, benchmark allowable cost, current cost, expected cost, life-cycle cost, target cost**.

cost deployment: See **quality function deployment**.

cost of quality: more accurately described as the cost of *non*-quality, this measurement reflects costs that a quality performance would have avoided. To determine cost of quality, a cost analysis is applied to various categories of internal failure costs (errors, waste, and unnecessarily long cycles) and external failure costs (misdeliveries and lost sales opportunities). See **business process tools** for links to other tools.

cost-plus pricing: an approach in which price is determined by adding a profit margin (the *plus*) over and above all the costs associated with producing a product or delivering a service.

cost reduction objective: the reduction of the difference between the **current cost** and the **allowable cost**.

CpK and Cp: metrics used to relate a variable's tolerance band (the numerator) to the actual spread of the distribution (the denominator). The CpK (process capability per thousand) tells how close a process is running to its *target* relative to the natural variability of the process. CpK will be high when you are meeting the target consistently with minimum variation. Cp (process potential) assumes the spread is within the tolerance band. CpK includes assumptions about the *centrality* of the variable within the tolerance band. In very simple terms, CpK will tell you the relationship between the size of a car, the size of the garage, and *how far away from the middle of the garage* you parked the car.

CQM: See **companywide quality management**.

craft production: the skilled craftsperson's practice of making things, one at a time. The craftsperson is usually a member of a regulated guild and is frequently assisted by apprentices. Also, the process of making the material objects of civilization as they were before the introduction of the division of labor at the beginning of the industrial revolution. By adding the element of employee involvement, lean production combines elements of craft production with the quantity output of mass production. Compare to **one-piece flow**.

cross-functional management: a method to manage the organization by using the combined expertise of individuals who represent several functional constituencies. These individuals form **cross-functional teams** that are the core of cross-functional management. Although members of these functional constituencies may have distinct targets and objectives, their shared vision is assured by the use of **policy management**.

cross-functional team: a team composed of representatives from several functional areas in the enterprise. These teams are the core of cross-functional management. See **team**.

current cost: the cost of a product as determined by the cost of its being manufactured today from existing components and production processes. See **cost** for links to variety of cost definitions.

curtain effect: a method that allows for uninterrupted flow of production regardless of external process location or cycle time. The primary factor for using the curtain effect is that an operation is best dealt with through the use of a batch. Sometimes a machine's physics, mechanics, or economics require a per cycle batch size, which then determines the curtain quantity. Sometimes the need to transport pieces will determine the curtain quantity. For example, a batch will be used when product must leave the cell for processing by equipment that cannot be put into the cell (heat treating, plating, etc.). Curtain quantities are established by dividing the per unit **cycle time** of the curtain process by the **takt time**.

customer: someone for whom a product is made or a service is performed. In a business there are internal and external customers. The *external customer* is the end user of a company's product or service, also known as the consumer. However, as each employee performs a service or creates a product (a report, a product component) that is received by another employee within the company, he or she is serving the *internal customer*. When applied to the supply chain, entire companies become customers of one another.

customer demand: how much product the customer wants and when the customer wants it. Available production time is divided by the rate of customer demand to determine **takt time**. Also called *demand*.

customer focus: attention to the customer's definition of **value** and the customer's criteria for products and services. Measuring the enterprise's success according to the level of customer satisfaction rather than other internal performance measures. (For example: measuring delivery success by how well the customer's requested delivery date is met instead of simple acknowledgement of delivery.) Some considerations of customer focus include who are our customers, what are their needs, what current features of our products or services do they value and what new features will they want, how do they rate us compared to our competitors and why, and how can we best keep them happy?

customer service index: a set of criteria that is developed to allow customers to rate the quality of a product or service on several different dimensions.

customer/supplier chain: the whole chain of connections required to produce and deliver a product or service to a customer. Continual feedback needs to occur back and forth all along the chain, which begins with the *suppliers of raw materials* and ends with the *consumer*. Compare to **supply chain** and **value chain**.

customer survey: any study carried out with the purpose of discovering what customers want or even might want that they haven't yet conceptualized. Also to get their feedback about what they are already getting, their ideas for improvements to current products and services, as well as their ideas for completely new products and services.

cybernetics: mathematician Norbert Weiner introduced this term to discuss communication, feedback, and control in systems. According to cybernetics, bureaucracies and factories are automated systems. According to Weiner, the system that can change its responses based on feedback is a system that learns. Although, first-order cybernetics was limited to observation of the *states* of a system, second-order cybernetics includes the observer as a participant in the system and uses chaos theory to look at how systems create and recreate their own boundaries. Cybernetic principles are useful to the lean enterprise because its success depends on how interactive it can be; that is, how quickly and effectively it can respond to feedback in its processes and from its customers—internal and external. Cybernetics is closely related to **systems theory** and they should be viewed as two facets of a single approach. See **system dynamics** and **systems thinking**.

cycle time: specifically, the time that elapses from the beginning of *one operation or one part of a process* until its completion. *Operator cycle time* is the total time for an operator to complete one cycle of an operation, including walking, loading, unloading, inspecting, etc. *Machine cycle time* is the time between when the "on button" is pressed until the machine returns to its original position after completing the operation. See **total cycle time**.

D

daily cell meeting: run by the supervisor of a cell, it is a short meeting to monitor daily work and reports, go over critical issues, share information from the management, and suggest improvement ideas.

decentralization: placing the authority and the right to make decisions as far down and as far out in the organization as possible. See **empowerment**.

decision tree: a graphic decision-making tool to analyze the costs and utility of alternative choices so that the best choices can be made. The decision tree diagram takes the collected data and uses symbols and diverging lines (branches) to show the impact or result of each choice. See **business process tools** for links to other tools.

dedicated line: a production line that serves the processing or assembly of only *one* part or product. Contrast with **joint line**.

defect: nonconformance in a product or part, or departure of quality from the intended effect. In **mistake-proofing** terminology, a defect is not the same as an error. A defect is *the result* of an **error**.

de-layering: removing excessive levels of supervision and management from the organization to delegate more decision-making to the level where the work is being done. See **empowerment**.

Delphi method or technique: a structured method of surveying a "jury" of experts to make a prediction and decide upon a plan. Anonymous questionnaires are circulated among experts for feedback. The process may be repeated several times for revisions and consolidation in order to arrive at a final forecast or plan.

demand: See **customer demand**.

demand flow: production by customer demand rather than to a predetermined schedule. See **pull production**.

Deming cycle: See **plan-do-check-act cycle**.

Deming management method: a management system developed by W. Edwards Deming that emphasizes the need for employee involvement and continued interaction among research, development, production, and sales departments to improve quality and satisfy customers.

Deming Prize: a quality award established in 1950 by the Union of Japanese Scientists and Engineers (JUSE) to commemorate the contributions to Japan of American quality pioneer W. Edwards Deming. The prize is given yearly to Japanese companies who have influenced the development of quality control and management in Japan. See **Deming, W. Edwards**.

Deming, W. Edwards: American quality pioneer credited with beginning the post-war industrial revival and quality revolution in Japan in the 1950s. He was a statistician whose methods contributed improvements to the 1940 census and to WW II military industrial improvements. It was Japanese business leaders who first reaped widespread benefit from his methods. They created the **Deming Prize** in appreciation. U.S. business woke up to his teachings in the 1980s and he became known as a leading quality guru in the U.S. Dr. Deming's business philosophy is summarized in his famous "fourteen points."

design for manufacture and assembly (DFMA): the explicit attention of cross-functional teams to the problems, concerns, and abilities of manufacturing when designing a product, often resulting in fewer assembly parts, mistake-proof or simplified assembly, greater ease in testing, and the avoidance of excessively high tolerances. The goal is to ease the manufacture of parts, making the manufacturing and assembly process more efficient and less costly.

design of experiment (DOE): a measurement tool that uses probability distribution to measure variable factors and interactions in systems to predict their most favorable outcomes. It identifies the factors and steps that are contributing the most to an observed variation in product specifications. One important use of DOE is to find the tolerances and nominal values, called parameter design, which will achieve design goals. The modern application of DOE involves the **Taguchi methods**.

design review (DR): the review by members of a team who have been through a particular design process to evaluate that process so as to carry the learning forward to improve the next design process.

DFMA: See **design for manufacture and assembly**.

diagnosis: a structured, strategic, and tactical process of identifying opportunities in the enterprise by means of self-evaluation, the baselining of critical functions, and the benchmarking of world class performance. The purpose of this process is to generate a consensual **gap analysis**.

A diagnosis differs from an **audit** primarily in two ways. First, a diagnosis is normally self-administered or administered by interested internal agents whereas an audit is administered by disinterested external agents. Second, a diagnosis is conducted in a spirit of helpfulness, as in a medical diagnosis, whereas an audit is conducted in a spirit of judgment to determine the "truth" of a situation, as in an accounting audit.

Dionysian management: encouraging the expression of enthusiasm, creativity, imagination, adventure, and comradery in the organization, which are valuable to teamwork and continuous improvement in the lean organization. Contrast with **Apollonian** and **Promethean management**.

discrete manufacturing industry: an industry where units such as cars or stereos are typically made by the assembly of a large number of component parts. Contrast with **process industry**.

division of labor: the breaking down of production processes into specialized, repetitive tasks suitable for workers with low skills. Originally referred to as the factory system. See **industrial revolution**.

DNA of Toyota: the essential matter of the Toyota Production System—the **scientific method**, which is the basis of the paradox of Toyota's seemingly rigid yet at the same time enormously flexible operations. In "Decoding the DNA of the Toyota Production System" (*Harvard Business Review*, September 1999), Steven Spear and Kent Bowen say that Toyota's operations are actually a continuous series of controlled experiments. When Toyota defines a specification, they are actually establishing a hypothesis that is then tested through action. This scientific method is not imposed on workers; it is ingrained in them. The authors describe four principles that show how Toyota sets up all its operations as experiments and teaches the scientific method to workers. "The first rule governs the way workers do their work. The second, the way they interact with one another. The third governs how production lines are constructed. And the last, how people learn to improve." Every activity, connection, and production path has built-in tests that signal problems immediately. This is the kind of commitment that makes a company a lean leader.

dock-to-dock time (DTD): the measure of the speed of materials through the factory—the time between the unloading of raw materials and the release of the finished goods for shipment. Also called *production dock to dock*. Dock-to-dock time is determined by dividing the total units built of the control part by the **end-of-line rate**. See **manufacturing measurables** for links to other measurables.

DOE: See **design of experiment**.

downtime: manufacturing time that is not useable because of equipment problems, lack of materials, lack of necessary information, or the unavailability of the operator.

DR: See **design review**.

draft target cost: the *expected cost* of manufacture determined by compiling the *projected costs* for each major subcomponent. This figure is used to determine whether the product can be produced and sold profitably. Contrast with **final target cost**. See also **target cost**.

drivers: the substantial forces impacting an organization's journey toward lean. Lean drivers include but are not limited to teams and teamwork, employee empowerment, continuous improvement, customer participation, change management, cycle time reduction, etc.

DTD: See **dock-to-dock time**.

E

early equipment management: one focus of **total productive maintenance**, this group of activities is directed toward obtaining optimal value-adding contributions from new equipment, which includes all phases of equipment management from design through vertical startup to obsolescence.

ecology of management: attention to the interconnections that exist within an enterprise as well as between it and the totality of its environment, including suppliers, competitors, customers, and supportive institutions. For example, while the company exists within and influences the society, societal values are also inside the enterprise and influence its daily operations.

economic order quantity (EOQ): the batch-sizing calculation resulting from a breakeven analysis in which both allocated changeover costs and inventory carrying charges are at their lowest point.

economic value added: this financial performance measure, a residual income measure determined by subtracting the cost of capital from net operating expenses after taxes, is closely linked to shareholder value. It creates a financial management and incentive compensation system that makes managers think and act like owners.

economies of scale: the reduction in unit costs that results from manufacturing products in higher *volumes*. Compare to **economies of scope**.

economies of scope: the reduction in unit costs that results from manufacturing a *range of similar items*. Compare to **economies of scale**.

effect: the result or outcome of a **cause** or causes.

EI: See **employee involvement**.

eight zeros: zero occurrence of the following eight problems in the workplace: waste, changeovers (minimal changeover time is the objective), downtime, defects, delays, loss, injuries, and customer dissatisfaction. Also, a *goal* that must be continuously aspired to.

emotional change curve: plots the typical way that individuals emotionally respond to change. Abrupt or forced change is initially met with (1) denial and resistance, (2) then anger, and (3) bargaining and negotiating. Change happens so rapidly in the lean organization that employees must be prepared for, motivated toward, and rewarded for change. Employees will then proceed to (4) tentative acceptance, (5) testing and adjusting, and finally (6) adopting and moving on with the change. When the company has not given some attention to the psychology of change, the bargaining and negotiating stage can end in poor morale, poor performance, and overt or covert disruption of change.

employee involvement (EI): the participation of employees at all levels in the continual improvement of products, processes, and systems necessary to become and remain world class. Employee involvement may occur on an individual basis but is optimal when used in a team-based environment. The degree to which employees are asked to participate can range from simply influencing a process to full control. Also called *total employee involvement (TEI)*. See also **empowerment**.

employee recognition programs: a variety of systems to provide incentive for and to reward employees for their exceptional work in supporting the organization's shared goals. These may be monetary or non-monetary, but a good system should be highly visible, fair, and consistent. The Business Research Lab says that in all the employee satisfaction studies they have conducted, they have never found high employee satisfaction scores in a firm with low employee recognition scores. See also **gainsharing**.

empowerment: the act of transferring portions of the decision-making process, as well as the authority to implement decisions, to employees. The extent to which empowerment can be given depends on the developmental maturity of the organization and its various groups.

end-of-line rate (EOL): the rate at which product comes off the production line. It is determined by dividing the units built per week of the control part by the plant production hours per week. As lean manufacturing evolves and process variations in performance are reduced, the time increment of weeks will change to days or shifts. See

manufacturing measurables for links to other measurables.

entrepreneurship: as applied to the lean organization, everyone is an entrepreneur in that every manager and employee is responsible for finding opportunities to expand the business by finding new ways to satisfy customers and new customers to satisfy.

EOL: See **end-of-line rate**.

EOQ: See **economic order quantity**.

equipment breakdowns: tool and machine breakdowns can occur because of lack of skills (no training in **autonomous maintenance**), defects in design (**early equipment management** not applied), deterioration not corrected (**preventive maintenance** not performed), and **standard operating procedures** not followed (improper oiling or calibration, etc.). See **total productive maintenance** for other initiatives to optimize equipment functioning.

equipment losses: See **six big losses**.

equipment repair history: a chronological listing of equipment defaults, repairs, and costs so that chronic problems can be identified and corrected, and economic decisions made.

ergonomics: the creation of transparent interfaces between people and their products to improve product ease of use and desirability. In the workplace, ergonomic knowledge of the human body is applied to the design of tools, machines, workstations, and the larger environment to optimize human performance while protecting safety and health.

error: an error is likely to occur when any of the conditions necessary for successful processing are wrong or absent. The resulting departure from correct performance causes a **defect**. Note that in **mistake-proofing** terminology, an error is not the same as a defect; an error *causes* a defect. Common manufacturing errors include missing a process step, performing an operation incorrectly, making a setup mistake, assembling parts incorrectly, using wrong materials, assembling in the wrong sequence, poor positioning of parts, poor equipment maintenance, tooling mistakes, etc.

error-proofing: See **mistake-proofing**.

ethics: considerations of right and wrong. The lean enterprise that wants to maintain its successes is assertively concerned with ethics as it considers the interests and well-being of all the principle stakeholders—customers, suppliers, owners, employees, and others. It will try to do the best it can for all and not just the least that is acceptable.

expected cost: the cost *predicted by product designers* who have no specific cost objective to meet but who are expected to minimize the cost of the product as it is designed. See **cost** for links to variety of cost definitions.

expert system: decision support software with the ability to make or evaluate decisions based on rules or experience parameters incorporated in the system's database.

extended team: this team is made up of members who provide special skills or expertise to the **core team** but who are not directly responsible for implementation.

F

factory within a factory: See **focused factory**.

failure mode and effects analysis (FMEA): the systematic analysis of a product in its planning, design, and manufacturing stages to ensure that its potential and logical failures are relatively uneventful; that is, the root causes behind mistakes are found and fixed so as to prevent recurrence before the product ever gets to the customer. The point of FMEA is to foresee and predict. Also referred to as *failure mode, effect, and criticality analysis (FMECA)*. See **failure mode and effects improvement**.

failure mode and effects improvement (FMEI): this is a *format* for conducting failure mode and effects analysis and generating improvement ideas. It is described by Ryuji Fukuda in *Building Organizational Fitness: Management Methodology for Transformation and Strategic Advantage* (Productivity Press). Used in conjunction with the SEDAC process, the FMEI format involves a "failure mode" column, a "known or predictable cause" column, and an "action item for countermeasure" column. Black and blue dots are used on failure mode and cause cards to indicate frequency and severity. Improvement cards are generated for evaluation and action. This combination of FMEA and SEDAC has been particularly successful for many companies. See **system for enhancing daily activities through creativity**.

failure reporting analysis and corrective action system (FRACAS): an action plan developed by a cross-functional team to track failure modes, equipment downtime, root causes, the implementation of corrective action, and status.

fault-tree analysis (FTA): a schematic review that takes a *backwards look* at failures, faults, defects, and shortcomings. Based on the hierarchy of relationship between causes and effects, it uses "and /or" function gates to find root causes. See **business process tools** for links to other tools.

FEI: See **focused equipment improvement**.

FFA: See **force-field analysis**.

final target cost: this cost is set at the *end of the product design stage* and, unlike the **draft target cost**, includes both the direct and indirect manufacturing costs. See also **target cost**.

firefighting: using emergency fixes to problems without attention to finding and fixing root causes.

first-look value engineering: the application of value-engineering principles to the major elements of product design to improve the capability of existing *functions*. Contrast with **zero-look** and **second-look value engineering**. See also **value engineering**.

first-pass quality (FPQ) rate: a core lean measurement that evaluates the percentage of an operation's (or a series of operations') ability to turn out product that

requires no more additional work than is defined on
the standard work sheet. It excludes all secondary
activities such as rework, manual adjustments, and
the like, from the core of the process. This measurement is essential to evaluating the robustness of the
process and its operations. See **manufacturing measurables** for links to other measurables.

first-tier supplier: a firm that provides direct supply to
another firm. See **second-tier supplier** and **third-
tier supplier**. These names basically indicate how
far away in the supply chain a supplier is from the
final assembly or product. They are largely a matter
of perspective. For example, Company B's first tier
supplier may be company A's second tier supplier.

first-time-through (FTT): the percentage of good units
completing any subprocess. It is determined by dividing the number of units *minus any defects* entering a
process point, by the total number of units entering
that process point. It can be used to measure sub-
processes in the path of a control part, the total
process of a given product, or the capability of the
plant. Compare to **first-pass quality rate**. See **manufacturing measurables** for links to other measurables.

fish-bone diagram: a problem or defect needing attention is written in summary form on the right side of
a chart (the effect side). A drawing resembling the
skeleton of a fish is placed on the left side of a chart
(the cause side). Each major diagonal bone of the
fish is labeled as a major category, often the **five Ms**.
Phrases suggesting causes of the problem are placed
on the small horizontal bones of the fish. The chart

effectively collects and summarizes solutions to a problem. See **cause and effect diagram with the addition of cards**.

five Ms: five words beginning with the letter "M" that describe the five areas of production in which quality problems can appear. The words are man (operator), machine, materials, methods (production information and standards), and mother nature (the environment).

five S (5S): an improvement process, originally summarized by five Japanese words beginning with S, to create a workplace that will meet the criteria of **visual control** and **lean production**. *Seiri* (**sort**) means to separate needed tools, parts, and instructions from the unneeded and to remove the latter. *Seiton* (**set in order**) means to neatly arrange and identify parts and tools for ease of use. *Seiso* (**shine**) means to clean and inspect. *Seiketsu* (**standardize**) means to require as the norm that everyone sort, set in order, and shine at frequent (daily) intervals to keep the workplace in perfect condition, and also to make use of **visual control systems**. *Shitsuke* (**sustain**) means to maintain the five S gains by training and encouraging workers to form the habit of always following the first four Ss. Also called *workplace organization and standardization* and referred to as the *five pillars of the visual workplace*. (Safety concerns are sometimes added to the process and referred to as the *sixth S*). See also **workplace scan**.

five S for safety: principles and activities that establish and sustain *safe conditions* in the workplace. These have been gleaned from years of 5S implementation and total quality control and combined with OSHA guidelines. Five S for safety focuses on eliminating causes of a rather substantial number of unreported near misses in the workplace, as well as minor and serious accidents. Safety techniques include but are not limited to color-coding, warning signs, lights and alarms, limit lines for storage, lines on the work floor to define passage, etc. Safety issues are sometimes referred to as the *sixth S*.

five whys: Taiichi Ohno's and Shigeo Shingo's practice of asking "why" five times whenever a problem was encountered. Repeated questioning helps identify the **root cause** of a problem so that effective countermeasures can be developed and implemented.

Here is an example of closing in on a problem with the five whys: (1) Why is there oil on the floor? Because oil leaks from the cylinder when it is activated. (2) Why does the oil leak? Because the o-ring is cut. (3) Why is the o-ring cut? Because the shaft is flawed. (4) Why is the shaft flawed? Because chips fly and adhere to the shaft. Also dirt in the oil abrades the shaft. (5) Why does dirt abrade the shaft? Because there are holes and gaps on the upper plate of the tank. *Solution:* Cover the openings on the upper plate of the tank to keep the shaft form being abraded.

flexibility: needed to survive and prosper in the lean management and manufacturing world, it is the ready capacity to adapt to new, different, and changing requirements. See also **cybernetics**.

flexible manufacturing system (FMS): an integrated production system having flexible, computer-controlled equipment that can change products, models, and volumes with minimal adjustments to accommodate rapidly changing product designs and small lot sizes.

flotilla: Peter Drucker's term for the "modules" in an advanced manufacturing system. These modules combine the standardization of command and control with the flexibility of process design and maneuvering.

flow: the progressive achievement of tasks as a product proceeds along the **value stream**, including design to launch, order to delivery, and raw materials into the hands of the customer without stoppages, scrap, or backflows. Flow can apply to the movement of information as well as material.

flow chart: a diagram used to show relationships among variables in a system such as machine layout, the placement of workers, and the flow of goods in a production process. Flow lines indicate the sequence of activities and special standard symbols represent particular operations. Also called *flow diagram*.

FMEA: See **failure mode and effects analysis**.

FMEI: See **failure mode and effects improvement**.

focus: See **policy**.

focus group: a small group of people—approximately six to twelve in number—called together to give their views on a particular subject such as a product, service, advertisement, plan, etc. The focus group provides a more qualitative kind of information than can be obtained by paper questionnaires or telephone surveys. It can be used to bring the company close to the voice of the customer and thereby help determine future product strategy. A focus group will ideally have a skilled facilitator to keep it on topic and distill key information. See **business process tools** for links to other tools.

focused equipment improvement (FEI): an approach, applied in the later stages of **total productive maintenance**, that focuses on specific equipment parameters or capabilities so as to improve **overall equipment effectiveness**. Key areas of focus include **breakdowns, minor stoppages**, speed loss, defect-free changeover, relationships between people and equipment, teamwork, and how to build in quality.

focused factory: the organization of the production facility, its management, and its support resources according to the market served, the customer base, and process similarities, the latter being the most important. This is usually a phased approach and is done logistically at first and then physically. **Cells** are important to the focused factory.

fool-proofing: the term "fool-proofing" (**baka-yoke** in Japanese) is considered offensive and should be avoided because it casts blame on the worker. See **mistake-proofing**.

force-field analysis (FFA): an examination of the change factors in an organization. All organizations have both *restraining forces*, which maintain the status quo, and *driving* forces, which lead toward change. If the restraining forces in an organization can be identified and understood, and then mitigated or redirected through force field analysis, change can be better managed. See **drivers** and **emotional change curve**. See **business process tools** for links to other tools.

FPQ: See **first-pass quality rate**. Also see **functionality/price/quality tradeoff**.

FRACAS: See **failure reporting analysis and corrective action system**.

FTA: See **fault-tree analysis**.

FTT: See **first-time through**.

full work: the work condition on the shop floor in which each operator is safely performing operations at **takt time** without any waiting.

function: the particular purpose for which a person or thing is specially fitted or designed or for which it exists. The domain of influence, which includes tasks and responsibilities, usually defines function.

functionality/price/quality (FPQ) tradeoff: When a buyer and supplier get together to determine if small adjustments in the buyer's quality and functionality specifications (but rarely price) can enable the supplier to achieve its target costs.

G

gainsharing: a system to provide financial rewards to large groups of managers and employees (this is beyond cell incentives) who work together on productivity and quality-improvement programs. A proportion of the measurable operational and financial gains are allocated to the managers and employees as a group. It is *not* profit-sharing in that gainsharing is tied to employee *performance*. Considerations in creating gainsharing programs are group composition, baseline performance, the gainsharing formula, and frequency of payouts. There are a variety of plans.

gap analysis: an analysis that compares current performance to desired performance so that solutions can be found to reduce the difference (close the gap). See **business process tools** for links to other tools.

gauge: any of a number of mechanical devices, common on the shop floor, that measure conformity or limits. See also **go/no go device**.

gauge repeatability and reproducibility (R&R) study: the evaluation of measuring instruments to determine whether they perform precisely. *Repeatability* is a report of variations in measurement obtained by one operator measuring one thing. *Reproducibility* is a report of the variations between more than one operator measuring one thing.

gemba: Japanese word of which the literal translation is "the real place." In the manufacturing field, gemba means the shop floor, where the actual product is being made, as contrasted to the office, where support services are provided.

go/no go device: a gauge used to *test* a machine against its upper and lower specification limits and determine whether or not the machine meets a criterion.

goodness of fit: demonstrated when a statistical technique indicates that data *does not* show **lack of fit** to a model but is instead a good match.

green belt: a team leader who has passed the first level of training in six-sigma improvement methodology and who can apply this learning to lead process or quality improvement teams *as part of* his or her regular job. See **black belt** and **master black belt**.

greenfield: a newer design or production facility where lean methods and best practice can be adopted and maintained from the very beginning. Contrast with **brownfield**.

group technology: See **cell design**.

H

hancho: a Japanese term meaning "group leader." (A *kacho* is a section manager and a *bucho* is a department manager. A *shusa* is a chairman of an investigation committee or the president of a board of examiners.

hanedashi: a device designed to automatically extract/eject the finished work piece from the machine so that the next part can be loaded. Operators then only need to pick up the ejected pieces and load. A component of **chaku-chaku**.

hard data: information that is quantitative, historical, and objective, usually the result of long and exhaustive studies having a numerical base. See **soft data**.

hazard and operability (HAZOP) study: an analysis, conducted by a team of people with varying backgrounds and expertise, that focuses on specific parts of a process, called "nodes," to identify hazards and operability problems. For each node, process parameters, intentions (using accompanying guidewords), and deviations are identified. Next, consequences of deviations are examined and safeguards and other appropriate recommendations are suggested. *Hazards* are defined as operations that could cause the release of toxic, flammable, or explosive chemicals; or any other action that could result in injury to personnel. An *operability problem* is any operation within the design envelope that could result in a viloation of environmental, health, or saftey regulations and/or cause a shutdown that would negatively impact profitablity. This analysis can be applied to new or existing processes in batch or continuous flow plants.

HAZOP: See **hazard and operability study**.

heijunka: a Japanese word that means "balancing" the amount of work to be done during a shift (the load) with the capacity to complete the work. It involves smoothing or sequencing orders evenly and in a repetitive pattern. Also called *load leveling*. See **level scheduling**.

heijunka box: a physical device used to level production volume and variety over a specified period (usually per day). The box visually displays a product family and is divided into slots that represent pitch increments. The slots are loaded with **kanbans** that represent customer orders. The order in which kanbans are loaded into the slots is based on volume and variety.

Herbie: Eliyahu Goldratt's term for a constraint in the production process. See **constraint**.

hidden factory: activities, people, and processes that produce waste and inefficiency. They have no value and are often overlooked within the metrics of a factory. Traditional financial and cost accounting systems can fail to identify the size and type of a hidden factory, which exists at the expense of profitability.

histogram: a bar graph that shows central tendency, process variability, and the relative frequency of collected data. With data typically taken from a frequency distribution, the histogram is very useful in providing a visual representation of how actual measurements or characteristics vary in regard to a target or specification value. See **business process tools** for links to other tools.

horizontal coordination: in a supply chain, the processes operating among firms in the *same tier* to maintain the value of the whole network. Contrast with **vertical coordination**. See also **first-tier**, **second-tier**, and **third-tier supplier**.

horizontal deployment: the implementation of a technique, method, or initiative across an organization on a given level.

hoshin: a Japanese term meaning a strong flash of insight that can influence policy. Literally, "shining needle," or "compass." Often translated as "policy" but perhaps the better translation is "strategy." A hoshin helps establish **strategic intent**.

hoshin kanri: means the "management" of a *hoshin*. Also called *hoshin management*. See **policy management**.

hoshin management: See **policy management**.

house of quality: an important process matrix for translating customer requirements and expectations into appropriate product characteristics. It ensures the integrated input as well as the aligned output of design, engineering, manufacturing, and marketing into the final product. Used by **cross-functional teams** for **quality function deployment**. See **business process tools** for links to other tools.

human computer-aided design: the next generation of **computer-aided design** (CAD) software. It can simulate the postures and movements of customers as they use a product to assess **ergonomic** design and function.

human qualities: personal qualities needed to succeed in the lean environment include flexibility, creativity, teamwork skills, a desire for quality and continuous improvement, a willingness to learn, and respect for people—both co-workers and customers.

human time (HT): the time required for manual operations. Also called *handling time*. Contrast with **machine time**.

hyperchange: the new change that surrounds us today. It is made up of three classical kinds of change—linear, exponential, and discontinuous—plus a new kind, chaotic change. In hyperchange, things appear and disappear abruptly. If we can meet the challenges of hyperchange with new attitudes and ways of functioning, particularly flexibility and quick response, we can manage it to help us drive continuous improvement.

I

implementation: the second stage in a three-stage change process, which becomes operative after pilot projects have proved their worth and have been adopted as a standard. See also **initialization** and **institutionalization**.

indirect manufacturing costs: manufacturing costs that cannot be traced directly to the product such as factory rent, maintenance wages, and depreciation of general production machinery.

industrial revolution: an extended period of growth in human productivity that began early in the 18th century by the introduction of the **division of labor**. In the late 19th century the introduction of steam powered mechanization, the cost of which was quickly reduced by the discovery of coal and then petroleum, led to a further acceleration of productivity. The term "industrial revolution" is commonly but mistakenly used to refer only to the introduction of steam power.

information age: a current period in our economic history in which the brokering of very large quantities of information, especially new information, by means of computers and high speed communications has become a basis of wealth and power. Compare to **knowledge era**.

information architecture: the flow of information within an organization, not limited to that contained in management information systems using information technology. Information architecture comprises *all* formal and informal information flows, especially those that are vital to quality, cost, and other production values. Compare to **just-in-time information** and **visual control**.

initialization: the first stage in a three-stage change process, which involves selling others on an idea and testing the idea. Also called *initiation*. Compare to **pilot**. See also **implementation** and **institutionalization**.

innovation: the novel application of technology to important problems. It can be conceptualized as "creative destruction." Because of the stubborn nature of paradigms, innovation frequently appears first on the "fringe" of the business community. However, with the right conditions, profitable companies with the right vision and culture can be successful at innovation, too. Innovation alone will not ensure success. The correct management and execution of new ideas, especially through **value-adding management** and **lean production**, is very important.

in-process inventory waste: the waste of having many unfinished products in process at the same time. See **waste**.

in-process kanban: See **kanban**.

inspection: the act of examining products or processes to ensure quality by comparing the actual outcome or result to what was expected. Inspection can only find defects that have already been generated by errors. In lean manufacturing, inspection is considered **waste**. Lean techniques attempt to *prevent* errors at their source. See **source inspection**.

institutionalization: the final stage in a three-stage change process, in which a change has been accepted as the standard procedure. See also **initialization** and **implementation**.

intangibles: the assets of a company that do not appear either on the balance sheet or the profit and loss statement, but which are nevertheless significant to the success of the company, particularly the lean enterprise. These assets include brand equity, intellectual property, human resources, leadership, business processes, and strategic relationships with customers, employee, suppliers, and government agencies. See **resource-based theory of the firm**.

integrated flow: See **one-piece flow**.

integrity level: the rating of a *machine's operating age* as opposed to its chronological age. A machine that works like a typical six-year-old machine may be actually be three years old and neglected, or twelve years old and very well maintained.

interorganizational cost investigation: the mutually beneficial trading of ideas and information about reducing costs among design teams from all the firms in a **target costing chain** so that all can achieve their **target costs**.

inventory: material on hand which may be categorized as raw material, work-in-process, or finished goods. One goal of lean manufacturing is to keep inventory levels to the minimum needed. Excess inventory is a form of **waste** in a lean manufacturing system.

inventory reduction: a cornerstone of the new manufacturing environment. Many just-in-time techniques are aimed at bringing inventories down, including raw material, work in process, and finished goods. There are a number of ways to measure inventory levels. Two are **stock turns** and number of days of stock.

invisible waste: the *intangible wastes* such as standby time that can go easily unnoticed without careful analysis of the production process. Contrast with **visible waste**. See **seven muda** and **waste**.

ISO 9000: ISO stands for "international organization for standardization." This ISO family of standards describes the *quality management of the processes* in which an organization goes about its work. They are not product standards — at least not directly. Nevertheless, the way in which the organization manages its processes is obviously going to affect its final product. *ISO 9001* describes quality management characteristics for an organization whose business processes range all the way from design and development to production, installation, and servicing. *ISO 9002* is for the organization that does production, installation, and servicing, but not design and development. *ISO 9003* is for the organization that does inspection and testing of final products and services. *ISO 9004* provides *guidelines* for developing and managing quality systems.

ISO 14000: This ISO family of standards focuses on *environmental management* or what the organization does to minimize the harmful effects of its activities on the environment, including its systems, auditing, labeling, environmental performance evaluation, and life cycle assessment. Beyond helping a company comply with environmental laws and avoid fines, ISO 14000 standards can help an organization save in the consumption of energy and materials, lower distribution costs, and improve its corporate image among regulators, its customers, and the public. An environmental continuous improvement effort will contribute synergy to a company's other continuous improvement efforts.

J

jidoka: Japanese term meaning "automation with a human touch." See **autonomation**.

Johari's window: a model used in training programs for giving and soliciting feedback, developed by psychologists Joseph Luft and Harry Ingham. Its four categories are "what I know about myself," "what I don't know about myself," "what others know about me," and "what others don't know about me." In the four-square grid, the "window pane" in which "what I know about myself" and "what others know about me" intersect is named the *Arena*. "What I don't know about myself" but "what others know about me" constitutes my *Blind Spot*. "What they don't know about me" but "what I know about myself" comprises my *Façade*. "What others don't know about me" and "what I don't know about myself" comprises the *Unknown*. (The window is sometimes referred to as *Joharry's window*.) Also modified for business practices as **window analysis**. See **business process tools** for links to other tools.

joint line: a production line that processes and assembles parts for more than one product. Contrast with **dedicated line**.

junjo-biki: Japanese term meaning a "sequenced withdrawal system." See **kanban**.

just-in-time: the first of the two major pillars of the **Toyota Production System** (the second being

autonomation), just-in-time is a system for producing and delivering the right items to the right place at the right time in the right amounts, eliminating buffer inventories. This technique approaches *just-on-time* when upstream activities occur minutes or seconds before downstream activities, so that one-piece flow is possible. The key elements of just-in-time are **flow**, **pull**, **standard work** (with standard work-in-process inventories), and **takt time**.

just-in-time information: a system for circulating information that follows the general principals of **just-in-time** production in which information vital to quality, cost, and delivery is provided to everyone who needs to know it in user-friendly format at the right place and at the right time.

K

kaikaku: Japanese term meaning the "radical improvement of an activity" to eliminate non-value-adding waste. An example would be reorganizing a product's processing operations so that it could go through its operations in one-piece flow in one short space instead of traveling to and from isolated process villages. Also called *breakthrough kaizen, flow kaizen,* and *system kaizen.*

kaizen: Composed of the Japanese *kai* meaning "to take apart" and *zen* meaning "to make good," kaizen is the gradual, incremental, and continual "improvement" of activities so as to create more **value** and less **non-value-adding** waste. Its success depends on the total commitment of the work force to increasing efficiency and reducing costs. Also called *point kaizen* and *process kaizen.*

kaizen costing: a lean-production accounting practice that uses cost reduction activities to achieve a target cost for each product, for each period. See **target costing**. Generally, direct material and labor costs are controlled through value engineering (and other engineering activities) and standard costing for each product. In contrast, overhead is managed primarily by budgeting and by *tapping employee know-how* via employee involvement methodologies such as total quality control (TQC) and total productive maintenance.

kaizen event: a planned and structured event that enables a group of associates to improve some aspect of their business. Prior to the actual event, an area is chosen and prepared, a problem is selected, leaders and teams are chosen, the problem is baselined, an improvement target is set, measurements are selected, and a timeframe is set for the event. The actual kaizen event aims for the quick, focused discovery of root causes and quick, focused implementation of solutions. These might be more accurately termed **kaikaku** or *breakthrough kaizen events*.

kaizen teian: Japanese term for "suggestion system." See **suggestion system**.

kanban: meaning "signboard" or "signal" in Japanese, a kanban is a type of **visual control** representing a certain quantity of material or parts. It might be a small traveling card attached to a box or cart, or an electronic signal sent by a scanned barcode. Being at the heart of **pull production**, a kanban signals upstream operations to deliver what is needed, in the quantity needed, when needed.

Many terms are used to describe kanbans. Basically, distinctions indicate different perspectives on the origin, destination, and function of a kanban. Many kanbans are *move* or *transport* kanbans in that they give permission for material to be moved from one place to another. A *withdrawal* kanban requests that material stored in one inventory location be delivered to a process step or other inventory location. A *replenishment* kanban is a request from an inventory location or a process step that the goods it has given up or used up be replaced. The *production* kanban tells a process step to produce the needed replacement material. A *supplier* kanban requests material from outside the internal process such as another division, plant, or even another company. An *in-process* kanban (IPK) controls the work-in-process (the amount of inventory allowed in a process). See also **triangle kanban**.

kanban card: this common signal for pull production will typically contain the following information: a picture and/or description of the part; what, when, and how much of the part to withdraw, make, or replenish; where the part has come from (the internal or external supply place); where it should go; and a material, part, subassembly, or assembly number.

kanban system: likened to an autonomic nervous system for **pull production**, the kanban system controls inventory amount and movement, authorizes production, provides visual control of operations and processes, and promotes production improvements. See **kanban**.

keiretsu: Japanese term for a group of companies that have formed an ongoing relationship based on their common traditions and business dealings for the purpose of gaining business advantages and strength. However, each maintains its operational independence. Some of these groupings are vertical, involving firms upstream and downstream from a system-integrating firm that is usually a final assembler. Some of these associations are horizontal, involving firms in different industries; for example, firms clustered around a financial institution that does financing for them while holding equity stakes.

key performance indicator (KPI): a tracking and monitoring index of the progress of daily management systems.

kingdom: a supplier network with only one **core firm**. This core firm is referred to as the *king*. Contrast with **barony**. See also **republic**.

knowledge era: a current period in our economic history when the acquisition and the application of practical knowledge to achieve the continuous improvement of product designs and production processes is considered to be an integral part of *every* employee's work. Compare to **information age**.

knowledge work: originally, the application of specialized knowledge in the **information age** and the service economy. Peter Drucker has pointed out that businesses are increasingly beholden to their **knowledge workers**, who alone possess the technology on which business is based. Technology, especially in the service economy, is the know-how, *not* capital equipment or even software. See **technology** and **innovation**. The term knowledge work should probably be broadened to include the work of continuous improvement that is characteristic of the **knowledge era**.

knowledge workers: persons who apply individual judgment when working with information, ideas, and knowledge, such as engineers, system analysts, personnel specialists, graphic artists, writers, publishers, etc. They are paid for the cognitive analysis they bring to their work as a result of advanced training and education as opposed to repeating routine processes.

kobetsu kaizen: Japanese terms meaning "focused improvement." See **focused equipment improvement**.

KPI: See **key performance indicator**.

L

lack of fit: the probability index that data will *not* fit a model, determined by any of a number of statistical techniques. Contrast with **goodness of fit**.

large-lot production: the manufacture of large quantities of the same item at a single window in time. Contrast with **small-lot production**.

lead time: the total amount of time required to get an order into the hands of the customer. It begins with *taking the order* and ends with *delivery to the customer*. Lead time and throughput time are the same when a scheduling and production system are running at or below capacity. Lead time exceeds throughput time when demand exceeds the capacity of a system and there is additional waiting time before the start of scheduling and production. Compare and contrast with **manufacturing lead time**, **processing time**, and **throughput time**.

leadership: a capable person's process of influencing others toward a continual realignment with a group's goals and strategies, in a way that fully respects their freedom. Good leadership is important to all levels and functions in the organization, from small teams on the shop floor to corporate board meetings.

lean: shorthand to refer to a lean manufacturing system, of which the Toyota Production System is the foremost example, that has relatively little

non-value-adding waste and maximum **flow**. The term has been used pejoratively to refer to anti-labor practices intending to reduce the number of workers within a company and to strong-arm tactics with suppliers.

lean engineering: See **concurrent engineering**.

lean enterprise: an enterprise with a total focus on waste elimination and the customer's needs, in all parts of its operations, manufacturing and administrative. Emphasis is given to lean structure and processes, flexibility of response, and methods and techniques to continually seize new opportunities as they arise. This enterprise is capable of producing high-quality products economically, in lower volumes, bringing them to market faster than mass producers.

lean equipment management: a **total productive maintenance** approach that ensures the efficiency, accuracy, and ease of operation and maintenance, as well as the readiness and availability of equipment and systems.

lean management: lean management systems vary from one organization to another, but all will include a scientific approach to waste elimination, individual ingenuity, teamwork, just-in-time information, a commitment to continuous learning and innovation, and an effective integration of their social and technical systems. See **value-adding management**.

lean management system: specifically, the nine-key lean management system set forth by Dr. Thomas

Jackson in *Implementing a Lean Management System* (Productivity Press). This continuous improvement system integrates an organization's long-term strategic planning with its day-to-day tactical improvement efforts. The nine keys of the system focus on the voice of the customer, effective leadership, the organizational structure, cooperative partnering, the distribution of information, a culture of continuous improvement, lean production, lean equipment management, and lean engineering.

lean measurables: metrics that are important to achieving, sustaining, and continuously improving a lean manufacturing environment. These may be *leading measurements* (measurements that drive improvement on a daily basis) or *trailing measurements* (measurements that track an improvement trend, usually performed at a higher level in the organization). Measurements may also be classified according to their use in the continuous improvement process, such as the *implementation level, tactical level,* or *strategic level.* Lean measurables are often different from and in sharp contrast to the traditional measures used to determine success in mass production. Also called *lean metrics.* See **manufacturing measurables**.

lean organization: See **organization architecture**.

lean production: a competitive advantage strategy of **just-in-time** production and the elimination of **non-value adding** wastes from the production process through the involvement of employees at all levels.

lean production system: a production system based on just in time and autonomation, with attention to the efficient integration of people, material, and machines by elements such as standard work, kanban, visual display, takt time, one-piece flow, and the pull system.

lean supplier network: a constellation of buyer-supplier relationships organized around one or more lead firms in which transactional protocols emerge based on lean supply principles. These protocols support sustained interaction and help lessen excessive competition among member firms, helping all to gain a network-based competitive advantage.

lean supplier relationship: a mutually beneficial affiliation between a lean buyer and lean supplier that is cooperative and stable.

lean thinking: a strong commitment to lean management and lean production, knowing that greater success can be achieved through the elimination of unnecessary waste throughout the entire business operation.

learning organization: an organization that is continuously learning from its environment and routinely discovering and fixing any important deviations from standardized expectations of performance, such as defects, equipment or process abnormalities, customer or employee dissatisfaction, and so on.

level scheduling: the sequencing of orders in a repetitive pattern, and the smoothing of day-to-day variations in total orders to correspond to longer-term demand. For example, if during a week customers order 200 of product A, 200 of product B, and 400 of product C in batches of 200, 200, and 400 respectively, level scheduling would sequence those products to run in the progression A, C, B, C, A, C, B, C, A, C. . . . Similarly, if a customer order totaling 1,000 products per week arrives in batches of 200 products on day one, 400 on day two, zero on day three, 100 on day four, and 100 on day five, the level schedule would produce 100 per day in the sequence A, C, A, B. . . . Some type of level scheduling is necessary at every producer, whether mass or lean, unless the firm and all of its suppliers have infinite capacity and zero changeover times. However, lean producers tend to create excess capacity over time as they free up resources. They work steadily at reducing changeover times so the short-term discrepancy between the heijunka schedule and actual demand is steadily minimized. They also practice **level selling**.

level selling: an attempt to create long-term relations with customers so that surges in production, often caused by the selling system itself (for example, quarterly or monthly sales targets) can be eliminated and production can instead be matched to anticipated future purchases by the customer.

levels of quality control: quality control efforts have varying levels of effectiveness and desirability. Control can come from (1) inspection by independent inspectors, (2) self-inspection by operators, or (3) successive inspection by the next operator in line. These first three methods focus on apprehending already defective product. More advanced quality control efforts aim to (4) inspect at the source to *detect errors* before they cause defects. The most advance type of quality control is (5) **mistake-proofing** or advanced techniques of upstream process control to *prevent errors*. See **error**.

levels of visual control: there is a logical progression to the effectiveness of visual control. The foundation of visual control consists of workplace organization and standardization (the 5S). The first level consists of the visual display of information; for example, how many products were made. The second level consists of sharing standards in the environment; for example, how many products were *supposed to be* made. The third level consists of actually building controls into the environment. The fourth level involves the use of *alarms* to indicate a particular event such as a breakdown. The fifth level uses methods to *stop defects* before they move further through the process. The sixth level uses methods to *prevent defects*. The top three levels constitute **mistake-proofing**. See **visual control**.

life-cycle cost: the total cost of a piece of equipment throughout its life, including design, manufacture, operation, maintenance, and disposal. See **cost** for links to variety of cost definitions.

Likert scale: a measurement method used in attitude surveys. Persons (customers, employees) are asked to choose a response, typically on a five to seven point scale, that ranges from "strongly agree" to "strongly disagree."

line balancing: the process by which work is evenly distributed to workers along the value stream to meet **takt time**.

linkages: the connections that take place between suppliers, manufacturers, distributors, retailers, and servicing in the value chain. It also refers to the connections within one firm between design, engineering, purchasing, manufacturing, marketing, and distribution. Managing linkages well is critical to the lean business environment.

linked kaizen costing: occurs when the cost-reduction objectives of the buyer's kaizen costing system are inputs to the supplier's **kaizen costing** system.

load leveling: See **level scheduling**.

load-leveling box: See **heijunka box**.

location indicator: a visual workplace element that shows where an item belongs. Lines, arrows, signboards, and shadowboards are some examples.

loss: the *forfeit of any opportunity to make a profit* because of the inability to meet customer demand. Tolerating **non-value-adding** waste is a major cause of loss of profit. In the field of total productive maintenance, loss is measured primarily in terms of lost production opportunities and is quantified in terms of time. For production losses see **six big**

losses. Production losses can also be categorized as **availabilty, performance**, and **quality losses**.

loss analysis: the practice of systematically quantifying and analyzing non-value-adding wastes to build a comprehensive loss picture. For example, overall equipment effectiveness is a comprehensive measure that can be used to compile an analysis of loss due to equipment problems.

lot: a volume of product that has been produced under similar conditions so that product within the lot is (expected to be) homogenous in all significant attributes.

M

machine time (MT): the time attributed to automated operations. Contrast with **human time**.

maintainability: the probability that a machine can be maintained in its stated operable conditions, or restored to them within a specified time, taking into consideration characteristics of design, installation, and operation. The basic measure of maintainability is **mean time to repair**.

maintenance prevention design (MPD): new equipment is designed and/or selected to ensure minimal and easy maintenance by incorporating feedback from users of current equipment. Also, life-cycle costs become an important consideration in equipment design or purchase.

major function: the part of the end product that performs a distinct secondary function such as an engine cooling system.

Malcolm Baldrige National Quality Award: named after economist Malcolm Baldrige, this government-sponsored award recognizes up to five American companies per year that demonstrate outstanding total quality management systems. The seven categories of the award criteria include leadership, strategic planning, customer and market focus, information and analysis, human resource development and management, process management, and business results.

management: the art/science/act of organizing, directing, and allocating the resources within a given
domain of control. Management is an *activity*, not a
position. We all practice it to a certain extent
regardless of our level in the organization. There
have been several significant changes in this field
during this decade. *First*, management science
applications were strongly impacted by Japanese
manufacturing innovations, which emphasized
redesigning the system rather than running the existing system in a better way. *Second*, management science models began to include quality achievement
objectives. Companywide efforts to attain total quality control (TQC) required cross-functionality and a
systems perspective. *Third*, management science
models began to network across many functional
databases as computers made information interde-
pendencies practical.

management accounting: in most companies, management accounting has not kept pace with the changes
occurring in manufacturing. Today's performance
measurement system must support the company's
manufacturing strategy in nonfinancial as well as
financial terms. While financial goals will be to
lower costs, achieve margins, get a return on assets,
or contribute to stock value, nonfinancial goals will
include quality, reliability, flexibility, innovation,
lead time, customer satisfaction, and social issues.

management by walking around (MBWA): leaders
make themselves visible and helpful by walking
around the shop floor and office to see what is going

on, listen, share ideas, and compliment efforts. The phrase was coined at Hewlett Packard, an early adopter of **policy management**. It is hard to imagine effective management by walking around unless policy has first been deployed. Otherwise there will be no obvious alignment of targets and activities to which the manager can add value by his or her visits.

manufacturing lead time: the amount of *manufacturing* time taken from the *issuance of raw material* through the production process to the *completion of the saleable product*. Compare and contrast with **lead time**, **processing time**, and **throughput time**.

manufacturing measurables: a number of measures that help set standards for performance in a manufacturing organization. A few are: **build to schedule, control part, dock-to-dock time, end-of-line rate, first-pass quality rate, first-time through, overall equipment effectiveness, production hours per week, volume, mix,** and **sequence**.

manufacturing resource planning (MRP II): a computerized system that expands **material requirements planning (MRP)** to include capacity planning tools, a financial interface to translate operations planning into financial terms, and a simulation tool to assess alternative production plans. MRP II helps support low volume, high variability environments.

mass customization: this new mental model of how a business can prosper by the production and distribution of *customized* goods and services on a *mass* basis *without* an increase in costs, generalizes the concept of value management to *all* corporate functions simultaneously—marketing and product design as well as manufacturing. It requires that new ways of managing be added to the new technologies. It has similarities to the concept of lean enterprise, but puts emphasis on managing the production of a variety of goods and services to meet the customer's individualized requirements.

mass production: the production of large numbers of similar products in a continuous process by an automated or semi-automated assembly line. Production is organized to exploit economies of scale and is managed by a military-style hierarchy governed by strict financial controls.

master black belt: individuals who have passed master-level training in six-sigma methodology and who are qualified to teach six-sigma improvement methodology in their organizations. As well as teaching six-sigma methodology to other employees, master black belts implement strategic improvements within the business, and coach and mentor other individuals who are leading improvement initiatives. See **black belt** and **green belt**.

material requirements planning (MRP): a computerized system used to determine the quantity and timing of supply of materials used in a production operation. MRP systems include a master production schedule, a bill of materials specifying each item needed, and information about current inventories from which to schedule the production and delivery of needed items. See **manufacturing resource planning (MRP II)**.

materials handler: a person on the production floor who paces the entire value stream to ensure that pitch and integrity are maintained by bringing material to the production line in a set route in set amounts for kanban replenishment. Because the operator does not have to leave the line, operator waiting time is made visible. The materials handler can also fill in for absent operators. Also called *mizusumashi, runner, water beetle, water spider,* or *whirligig.*

matrix diagram: used to chart corresponding elements involved in a situation or event. Elements are arranged in rows and columns on a chart. Intersection points show the presence or absence of relationships among pairs of elements. Problem solving and continuous improvement is facilitated at the intersection points, also referred to as idea conception points. Types of matrices are the L-type (checks for relationships between two sets of items, A to B), the T-type (two L matrices combined to check for A to B and A to C), the Y-type (checks for interactions among three sets of items, A to B to C to A), the X-type (checks four sets of items, A to B to C to D to A), and the C-type (a cube that can check for linkages between A, B, and C). See **business process tools** for links to other tools.

MBWA: See **management by walking around**.

mean time between failures (MTBF): a rating that indicates the average ability of an item or system to perform a required function, under stated conditions, without failure, for a stated period of time. It is determined by dividing the timeframe being analyzed by the number of breakdowns. It is a **reliabilty** rating.

mean time to repair (MTTR): a rating that indicates the average time (rapidity and ease) in which maintenance operations can be performed to either prevent malfunctions or to correct them if they occur. It is determined by dividing the total downtime for repairs by the number of repair incidents. It is a **maintainability** rating.

measurement: a numeric value used to indicate a level of accomplishment or a rate of improvement toward a targeted goal. See **lean measurables** and **manufacturing measurables**.

measurement cycle: an effective measurement system will cycle upon itself. It will (1) baseline current performance, (2) identify critical gaps and opportunities, (3) measure efforts to close those gaps and seize those opportunities, and (4) set new targets.

menu: a selection of functional options in a software display.

metric: a measurement. See **measurement, lean measurables, manufacturing measurables**, and **visual metrics**.

milestone chart: a detailed activity chart used by a deployment team to indicate when and by whom implementation events are to occur. Teams can

create these charts for their specific activities and
use them to help guide the change process.

milk run: the routing of a supply or delivery vehicle to
make multiple pickups or drop-offs at different loca-
tions. Milk runs are made by suppliers or cooperat-
ing groups of suppliers who make frequent, small
deliveries to customers who practice just-in-time.
The route of a **materials handler** within a factory is
also called a milk run.

minor abnormalities: abnormalities that tend to be
ignored but that can lead to unwanted **minor stoppages** and defects. Minor abnormalities include dirt,
grime, small amounts of wear, scratches, play, loose-
ness, leaks, corrosion, deformation, cracks, vibration, and excess heat.

minor stoppages: these occur when equipment tem-
porarily idles or shuts down due to a small problem.
Minor stoppages particularly reduce the effectiveness of automated processes that could otherwise
run attended. They are not taken as seriously as
breakdowns because the size of the loss isn't obvious. They typically last only a few seconds, such as
when product components snag on a conveyor line.
We usually treat the surface symptoms and don't
observe, inspect, or problem solve. However, minor
stoppages can lead to more serious breakdowns.
Autonomous maintenance can prevent or minimize minor stoppages.

mission statement: an organization's *statement of
purpose* that may include a business definition, a

definition of customers, strategies, goals, main measures, and values. It should be a written, clearly expressed, and motivational statement. An exemplary mission statement will include the implicit or explicit intention of making a contribution to the economy, society, or to human advancement and well-being. See **vision**.

mistake-proofing: an improvement technology that uses a device or procedure, also called a *poka-yoke*, to prevent defects or equipment malfunction during order-taking or manufacture. For example, in order-taking, a computer screen can be formatted to accept traditional ordering patterns and question any orders outside the pattern. In manufacturing, a set of photocells can be embedded in containers moving along an assembly line to prevent components with missing parts from progressing to the next stage. If an operator's hand does not break a light beam in the container by handling the part in the container, the container will not move to the next station. **Mistake-proofing devices** are important to the production line in several ways: They (1) enforce correct operations by eliminating choices that lead to incorrect actions, (2) signal or stop a process if an error is made or a defect created, and (3) prevent machine and product damage. Compare to **autonomation**. See also **levels of visual control**.

mistake-proofing development chart: a wall chart used to structure and display the mistake-proofing process. The chart has places to describe a defect, tell its location and rate of occurrence, and list all the deviations from standard. There is also a section for analysis (the five whys) to determine root causes, a section for ideas to prevent the defect, and a section to record the testing of ideas.

mistake-proofing devices: mechanisms to prevent errors and defects in manufacturing processes. Common categories of devices include (1) guide and interference rods or pins, (2) templates, (3) limit and micro switches, (4) counters, (5) odd-part-out methods, (6) sequence restrictors, (7) standards, (8) critical condition indicators, (9) delivery/detection chutes, (10) stoppers and gates, (11) sensors, (12) and quality controls of the mistake-proofing devices themselves.

mix: a metric that is used in the **build-to-schedule** formula to determine how well customer product specifications are being met. Mix is determined by dividing the number of units built to mix by the units scheduled or produced (whichever is less). Mix generally means product variety.

mixed-model production: a production process that can turn out a "family" of related products in a random order and in a wide range of quantities without needing line changeovers or resetting. See **dedicated line** versus **joint line**.

mizusumashi: See **materials handler**.

monument: any design, scheduling, or production machine or tool with a physical constraint or equipment scale that makes it very difficult and costly to move, which means that designs, orders, and products must be *brought to* the machine or tool *in batches*. This means that materials must wait in queue for processing. Contrast with **right-sized tool**.

MPD: See **maintenance prevention design**.

MRP: See **material requirements planning**.

MRPII: See **manufacturing resource planning**.

MT: See **machine time**.

MTBF: See **mean time between failures**.

MTTR: See **mean time to repair**.

muda, mudi, and mura: Japanese terms meaning respectively waste, inefficiency, and inconsistency. See **seven muda** and **non-value-adding**.

multi-machine handling: when an operator handles *more than one machine* of a similar type. Also called *multi-equipment handling*. Contrast with **multi-process handling**.

multi-process handling: a production process in which employees operate and maintain *different types of production equipment* and perform a *variety of functions* within a cell or cells. Multi-process handling is essential in production cells with many types of machines. It ensures worker flexibility, causes less fatigue, and permits easy adjustments to fluctuations in demand. See **multi-machine handling**.

N

network infrastructure: technical seminars and training programs, consulting services, interorganizational problem-solving efforts, and any other arrangements that help to improve the capabilities of a cooperative network.

network protocols: rules for behavior that apply to a network of firms. Their purpose is to minimize the negative potential of excessive competition among firms in the network.

noncompliance: the result of an activity, product, or document not meeting the intent of a policy, procedure, or instruction. See **audit**.

non-value-adding: any operation or activity that takes time and resources but does not add **value** to the product or service sold to the customer. Contrast with **value-adding**.

O

Occupational Safety and Health Administration (OSHA): The U.S. government agency within the Department of Labor that overseas health and safety regulations for U.S. industries. Besides establishing standards, which were established as law in the OSHA Act of 1970, it supports research and provides, information, education, and training in safety issues.

OEE: See **overall equipment effectiveness**.

OEM: See **original equipment manufacturer**.

office: a collection of people, tasks, processes, procedures, information, instructions, equipment, and physical layout. In a manufacturing company, the office should be applying lean principles to support the lean efforts of the plant.

Ohno, Taiichi: Japanese business leader credited with developing the **Toyota Production System**, widely recognized and copied throughout the world. Also considered by some to be the "father" of the kanban system because of his observation of supermarket operations on a visit to the U.S. in 1956 and his subsequent work regarding continuous supply of materials to supermarket shelves. Ohno was a distinguished graduate of the Nagoya Institute of Technology and former Executive Vice President of Toyota Motor Company. See **five whys** and **seven muda**.

on-error training: training that is performed as part of a postmortem process to anticipate and avoid future error conditions, in which **one-point lessons** can be used to advantage.

one-piece flow: the manufacturing process in which *product flows without waiting* through various operations in design, order-taking, and production without backflows, scrap, or the need for excess inventory. Also called *single-piece flow*. Contrast with **batch-and-queue**.

one-point lesson: a short and focused visual presentation sharing just-in-time information to improve performance. Information is presented in "bite sized" chunks, when and where it is needed. One-point lessons may be categorized as to their intent. A *basic* one-point lesson fills some knowledge gap. It might show how to replace oil in a machine. A *problem case study* one-point lesson follows on the heels of a breakdown, defect, or abnormality to teach how to prevent it from happening again. An *improvement case study* one-point lesson summarizes the results of team improvement activities for all to see. One-point lessons might be posted on a wall near a machine, collected in a notebook, etc. Also called *single-point lesson*.

one-touch exchange of die (OTED): minimizing changeovers to the point where they can be performed in *less than one minute or with a single touch*. It is the next level to aspire to after SMED (single-minute exchange of die) changeovers of less than ten minutes have been achieved. Compare to **single-minute exchange of die** and **zero changeover**. See also **changeover**.

open-book management: a management approach in which financial information relevant to design, scheduling, and production activities is shared with all employees of the firm, and with suppliers and distributors up and down the value chain.

operation: an activity or activities performed on a product by a *single* machine or person. Contrast with **process**.

operator balance chart: used to visually display work elements, times, and operator assignments at each operation in the value stream. It can reveal opportunities to improve total cycle time.

organization architecture: the structure and the dynamic relationship between and among the various parts of an enterprise involving the responsibilities of those parts to other parts of the organization and the relationship of those parts to the value stream.

organizational learning: the continual learning that must occur in a lean organization in order to acquire new skills and technologies. Also, the structures and processes of acquiring that learning.

original equipment manufacturer (OEM): a company that uses product components from one or more other suppliers to build a product that it sells under its own company name and brand. The term has also been mistakenly used to refer to a component supplier. One and the same company can supply components to other companies and also buy components from other suppliers to build its own products. An example is IBM.

OSE: See **overall supplier effectiveness**.

OSHA: See **Occupational Safety and Health Administration**.

outsourcing: the contracting of production of goods or delivery of services with an outside vendor, allowing a company to focus on its core competencies. Outsourcing can reduce inventory, promote better capacity use, and make personnel allocation more flexible. However, working with partners has its own set of challenges. The need for accountability puts a premium on good communications.

overall equipment effectiveness (OEE): the measure of a single piece of equipment's actual contribution as a percentage of its potential to add value to the value stream. Overall equipment effectiveness = availability *x* performance *x* quality rate, *x* 100. It is the primary metric of **total productive maintenance**.

To calculate the *availability rate*, divide the operating time by the net available time and multiply that result by 100. To calculate the *performance rate*, multiply the ideal cycle time by the processed amount. Divide that number by the operating time. Then multiply that number by 100. To calculate the *quality rate*, first determine the processed amount minus the defect amount. Divide that number by the processed amount. Then multiply that number by 100. See **manufacturing measurables** for links to other measurables.

overall supplier effectiveness (OSE): the cost of doing business with suppliers in terms of quality, cost, and delivery. OSE = percent of defects (quality performance) x cost variances (cost performance) x percent of missed deliveries (delivery performance).

P

paced withdrawal: a method of leveling that involves moving small batches of material through the value stream over time intervals that are equal to the **pitch**.

pack-out quantity: a small batch equal to the number of parts/units that can be moved through the value stream in an efficient flow. While takt time is customer driven, pack-out quantity may or may not be. See **pitch** and **takt time**.

paradigm: a fundamental idea about reality, frequently unquestioned and difficult to change, that conditions all our thinking about and even our physical perceptions of the world or some aspect of experience. Paradigms about running a business include assumptions about mass production, innovation, selling, management, stakeholders, systems, and marketing. For example, when confronted with a problem, a traditional manufacturing paradigm will cause us to ask "who" and defect control will focus on inspection. A lean paradigm will ask "why" and defect control will focus on prevention.

The following are examples of paradigms that were too limiting—also known as famous last words: (1) "Heavier than air flying machines are impossible." Lord Kelvin, c. 1895. (2) "I think there is a world market for about five computers." Thomas J. Watson, 1943. (3) "With over fifty foreign cars already on sale here, the Japanese auto industry isn't likely to carve a big slice out of the U.S. market for itself." *Business Week*, 1968,

paradoxical thinking: instead of forcing a choice between opposites, an attempt is made to integrate the benefits of both.

parallel hub collaboration: simultaneous, bi-directional communication among all supply chain partners who are sharing a single database of information. Contrast with **point-to-point serial communication**.

parallel lines: two productions lines laid alongside one another.

Pareto chart: named after European economist Vilfredo Pareto, this bar graph separates and displays the "critical few" from the "trivial many" causes of a problem. A relatively small number of causes (about 20 percent) usually accounts for a large proportion of the problems (about 80 percent). The chart arranges bars from left to right in descending order of importance and shows the cumulative percentage of each. As an improvement tool, it helps you determine where to focus your efforts to get the most return. See **business process tools** for links to other tools.

Pareto principle: this statement postulates that 80 percent of an observed effect is due to only 20 percent of the observed causes. Although usually expressed as an 80/20 rule, these numeric values are not absolute. It is a general principle of concentration, inequality, and inverse proportion. It reminds us that the relationship between inputs and outputs is not balanced and calls attention to disproportions so that corrective actions can be taken.

part-quantity analysis (P-Q analysis): the ratio that expresses the total end items sampled to the total volume. It can be used to find the relationship between the products being produced and their share of the business. It is used in creating focused factories as well as cellular processes. It is also used in conjunction with routing analysis to surface part-path similarities and in selecting key product families as a focus for value stream maps.

part-specific capacity worktable: a worktable that shows the processing capacity of each machine in a production line.

pay-on-receipt: a transaction in the supply chain where the buyer pays the supplier upon receipt of goods without the supplier having had to prepare statements or invoices for the buyer.

PDCA cycle: See **plan-do-check-act cycle**.

PdM: See **predictive maintenance**.

percent-loading chart: used to identify under-utilization of operators, the chart furnishes information for more detailed analysis by displaying each process step's cycle time in relation to the end-of-line rate. Operator requirements can be determined by dividing the sum of all the cycle times by the end-of-line rate.

percent yield: the number of acceptable parts that pass through a given process step as a percentage of the total number that enter the process step.

perfection: the complete elimination of non-value-adding waste so that all activities along a value stream create **value**.

performance analysis or performance measures board: See **control board**.

performance loss: also referred to as *speed loss*, this loss occurs due to to reduced operating speed and minor stoppages. Contrast with **availablity loss** and **quality loss**. See also **six big losses**.

pick-up/set-down waste: wasted movement resulting from locating worktables away from a conveyor line, causing workers to carry pieces from the conveyor to their work tables and then back again. Compare to **point of use**. See **seven muda**.

pilot: an experimental task or exercise to determine the viablity of a project or product. Compare to **initialization**.

pitch: the adjustment to **takt time** that allows work to flow more evenly on the shop floor. It ensures that a manageable amount of **pack-out quantity** of the work in process is released to a downstream operation. Pitch is determined by multiplying takt time *x* pack-out quantity.

plan-do-check-act cycle (PDCA): a cycle that represents four steps used in many improvement activities. It encompasses planning, doing, checking results, adjusting, and then planning again. Also known as the *Shewhart cycle* after Walter Shewhart, a statistician in the Bell Laboratories who developed it, and the *Deming cycle*, after W. Edwards Deming who advocated its use. See **business process tools** for links to other tools.

plant within a plant: See **focused factory**.

platform: See **product family**.

PM: See **preventive maintenance**.

P/O matrix: See **policy and objectives matrix**.

point of use: the condition in which all supplies are within arms reach and positioned in the sequence in which they are used to prevent extra reaching, lifting, straining, turning, and twisting. Compare to **pick-up/set-down waste**.

point-to-point serial communication: a single, direct communication link between two trading partners that lacks visibility of the other links along the supply chain. Contrast with **parallel hub collaboration**.

poka-yoke: Japanese term used by Shigeo Shingo to mean "innocent mistake-proofing." See **baka-yoke** and **mistake-proofing**.

policy: an improvement theme with a set of team charters that extends traditional strategy into implementation by aligning top management and, through policy deployment, the entire company, to three to five of the company's strategic improvement objectives. See **policy management**.

policy and objectives matrix (P/O matrix): an x-type matrix used for strategic planning that shows organizational policies (strategies/goals), objectives (initiatives/projects), measures (targets/milestones), who is responsible (teams/individuals/departments), the impact on the organization (cost/benefit, financial/non-financial), and the relationship between each of these factors. This is all done on one large piece of paper. Also called *planning and objectives matrix*. See **policy definition, policy deployment, policy management**, and **matrix diagram**.

policy definition: the process of establishing a policy, frequently employing an x-type matrix. Policy definition includes identifying critical short-term gaps, choosing measures, identifying goals, and determining financial impacts.

policy deployment: the process of cascading or communicating a policy from top to middle management through a give-and-take process called **catchball**. In some companies, catchball includes supervisors and team leaders: See **policy management**.

policy management: strategic decision-making by a firm's executive team to focus resources on the critical initiatives needed to achieve the firm's overall business objectives. Using a visual matrix similar to ones used for quality function deployment, three to five key objectives are selected while all others are clearly *deselected*. Selected objectives are then translated into specific projects and deployed down to the implementation level. Policy management unifies and aligns the firm's resources and establishes targets against which to measure progress toward key objectives on a regular basis. Also called *strategy management*. See also **policy deployment**.

P-Q analysis: See **part-quantity analysis**.

precision maintenance: a highly focused approach to machine upkeep that is characterized by highly detailed maintenance instructions.

predictive maintenance (PdM): a maintenance component of **total productive maintenance** that is based on *machine history and data-based equipment knowledge*. Measured physical parameters are applied against known engineering limits to dictate the replacing or servicing of components so that breakdown and malfunction are reduced. Maintenance is usually tied to hours run, pieces made, or cycles performed. The index will change depending on the machine component being focused on. For example, constant drive motors will be indexed to the number of hours run whereas dies and presses will be indexed to cycles or pieces. Compare to **preventive maintenance**.

preventive maintenance (PM): a maintenance component of **total productive maintenance** that is based on the *critical operating characteristics* of the equipment and the acceptable operating ranges for those characteristics. Machine maintenance is scheduled at predetermined intervals to achieve smooth, continuous operation. Critical operating characteristics include, for example, oil viscosity, motor vibration, current draw, etc. Compare to **predictive maintenance**.

problem statement: as applied to problem solving and process improvement or as used in a CEDAC chart, a good problem statement should be a comparative statement that *quantifies* the effect of some problem occurring within a particular time period. It should be short and focused. An example is: "In the period between xx and xx, defects from line A have increased from 4 per shift to 12 per shift, causing a waste of materials and extra time on inspections." Compare to **target statement**.

process: a sequence of operations (consisting of people, machines, materials, and methods) for the design, manufacture, and delivery of a product or service. Contrast with **operation**.

process capacity: the number of work pieces a machine can produce in a day, calculated by dividing the working hours in a day by the total work piece processing time (which is the sum of the processing time and any changeover time.) Also called *capacity figure*.

process capacity table: a form used in cellular manufacturing to determine the daily capacity of all the operations in a process by recording all its parts in some detail, including sequence of operations, walk time between operations, manual work time, machine time, time per piece per machine, etc. Some of the "numbers" used in the process capacity table are taken from the **time observation sheet**. See **standard work combination sheet**.

process design analysis sheet: used to improve **cell design,** this form documents the current versus proposed measures in terms of floor space, part path, number of operators required, standard work in process, manufacturing lead time, and value-adding ratio.

process industry: an industry characterized by continuous operations or treatments in manufacturing, executed in a definite sequence. Some batch operations take place in process industries. In either case, a limited number of raw materials are processed to produce numerous variations of a limited number of product types. Contrast with **discrete manufacturing industry.**

process mapping: the attempt to understand the flow of activities and each individual activity within the context of an entire process. Process maps can target a single process or link cross-functional processes. A good process map generates improved understanding of a process and its relationship to the overall business, and surfaces constraints, opportunities, and tradeoffs. A good process map enables people unfamiliar with the process to understand the interplay of activities during the workflow. See **business process tools** for links to other tools.

process razing: the total restructuring and improvement of layout in processing and assembly operations.

process route analysis table: a table used to group similar production processes into families of processing operations.

process village: a grouping of machines or activities according to the type of operation being performed. Examples of process villages are the grinding area and the order-entry area. Contrast with **cell**.

processing time: the time a product is *actually being worked on* in design or production. Processing time is typically a small fraction of **throughput time** and **lead time**. See also **manufacturing lead time**.

product family: a related range of products sharing equipment and processing attributes that allows them to be produced interchangeably in a production cell. Also called a *platform*.

production hours per week: a measure of plant production hours, which includes weekend work but excludes break time and lunch time. See **manufacturing measurables** for links to other measurables.

production kanban: See **kanban**.

production smoothing: See **level scheduling**.

productivity: the ratio of outputs to inputs of labor and/or other resources, stated in real terms (free of inflation effects).

profit: the residual of total revenues from the sale of a
product less the total cost of all factors associated
with its production, including labor, materials, management, and capital. Aside from any accounting
notions of profit (the meanings of which are sometimes obscure), a business is profitable if it returns
to its investors more than enough to prevent them
from seeking better returns elsewhere.

profit management: the management of operations to
achieve a precise target profit rate through the application of target costing for new products and kaizen
costing of existing products and operations. The
term **target costing** is sometimes used as a synonym
for profit management.

Promethean management: management that is
forward-looking, future-focused, ambitious, and
innovative. These are valuable qualities for setting vision and mission, and for supporting
continuous improvement in the lean organization. Contrast with **Apollonian** and **Dionysian
management**.

pull production: a system of production and delivery
instructions in which nothing is produced by the
upstream supplier until the downstream customer
signals a need. Pull can operate with single units or
small batches. It enables production without preset
schedules. Contrast with **push production**. See
also **kanban**.

push production: conventional production in which
production schedules are pushed along based on

sales projections and availability of materials. It leads production employees to make as much product as they can as fast as they can, even if the next process is not ready to use the materials, which causes large work-in-process inventories. Contrast with **pull production**.

Q

quality chart/table: a matrix that is used in quality function deployment to relate various ways of assessing the product or service to one another. For example, customer demands versus mechanisms, mechanisms versus tests, tests versus failure modes, failure modes versus customer demands, etc. Purpose may vary from chart to chart but the common goal is to look into the nature of the product or service and see what might be done to improve it. See **house of quality**. See **business process tools** for links to other tools.

quality circles: small, face-to-face groups, usually of ten or fewer members such as employees and/or managers who get together at frequent intervals to work out solutions to quality, service, cycle time, and productivity issues. Also called *improvement teams, quality teams,* etc.

quality function deployment (QFD): a decision-making process that adds the voice of the customer to product development. By using a customized **house of quality** matrix, multi-skilled project teams reach a common understanding about the voice of the customer and consensus on the final engineering specifications of the product. This process integrates the perspectives of team members from different disciplines, focuses their efforts on resolving key trade-offs in conformance to product targets, deploys their decisions through successive levels of detail, and eliminates expensive backflows and rework near launch. The house of quality matrix helps the team weigh quality levels, customer expectations, benchmark data, target values, technical requirements, manufacturing parameters, etc. Also called *cost deployment.*

quality loss: also referred to as *defect loss*, this loss occurs due to scrap, rework, and the defects that are produced during startup (some companies count their startup losses as availability/downtime loss). Contrast with **availabilty loss** and **performance loss.** See aslo **six big losses.**

quality maintenance: an approach to the maintenance of equipment using the concept of zero defects. The goal is not to have equipment that is simply running but equipment that is calibrated to make a quality product.

queue time: the time a product spends waiting in a line for the next step in design, order processing, or fabrication.

quick changeover: a process that focuses on reducing **changeover time.** See also **changeover.**

QS-9000: A standard containing all of ISO 9001 but adding requirements and information specific to U.S. automotive companies (being adapted internationally). See **ISO 9000.**

R

R&R study: See **gauge repeatability and reproducibility study**.

RCM: See **reliability-centered maintenance**.

real time: time that is directly observable and measurable.

red-flag conditions: conditions in the manufacturing process that often provoke errors. These may include adjustments; tooling and tooling changes; dimensions, specifications, and critical conditions; many or mixed parts; multiple steps; infrequent production; ineffective standards; mistaken symmetry/asymmetry, rapid repetition; high volumes; and environmental conditions such as housekeeping, poor lighting, air quality, materials handling, etc.

red tag: a tag applied to items in an area targeted for improvement—production or administrative—for which there is no obvious use. This may also include excess amounts of useable items. Tagged items are moved to temporary storage in a *red-tag holding* area to give workers from other areas the chance to claim items that may be useful to them. After a specified time red-tag items are disposed of. Red tagging is an initial step in the process improvement method called 5S. See **five S**.

reengineering: the analysis and redesign of business processes to achieve dramatic improvements in performance through the use of current information technology. Reengineering seeks to minimize waste and to more closely align tasks, responsibilities, and skills to better serve the recognized value stream. It focuses on innovative ways to do business, managing people through changes, and using appropriate information technology to support new environments.

reliability: the probability that machinery and equipment can perform continuously without failure for a specific interval of time under stated conditions. The basic measure of reliability is **mean time between failure**.

reliability analysis: identifying the maintenance needs of significant items and classifying them with respect to malfunction on safety, environmental, operational, and economic bases. Subsets of reliability analysis are **failure mode and effects analysis**, **fault-tree analysis**, and the **hazard and operability study**.

reliability-centered maintenance (RCM): optimizing maintenance intervention and tactics to meet predetermined reliability goals.

reliable methods: activities made up of those elements that, when followed, will cause predictable and desirable results, and that, when not followed, will result in predictable defects or waste.

reorder point: the level of inventory that must be maintained to insure that stock is available to meet average daily demand. When stock drops to the reorder point, a new order is made to replace the used stock. The reorder point belongs to an automated inventory management system called *reordering point method*, a statistical method that allows factories to order the same amount of parts or products each time. A **kanban system** uses this process. See **kanban** and **triangle kanban**.

repeatability: this variability value is determined by a number of measurements with the same instrument by the *same appraiser* on the same characteristic. Contrast with **reproducibility**.

replenishment kanban: See **kanban**.

reproducibility: this variability value is determined by a number of measurements with the same instrument by *different appraisers* on the same characteristic. Contrast with **repeatability**.

republic: a supplier network that has no **core firm**. See **barony** and **kingdom**.

resource-based theory of the firm: an economic theory whose major hypothesis is that the competitiveness of the business firm depends upon how well its leaders develop the firm's resources, in particular its core competencies and other intangible assets. The theory helps explain the success of lean companies because the types of investments required to implement lean production and lean enterprise are largely investments in the intangible assets of people, processes, and relationships. See **intangibles**.

retains: physical objects used as records for an audit.

return-address: See **address**.

rework and defect waste: the waste of having many products that must be either reworked or discarded. See **seven muda** and **waste**.

right-sized tool: a design, scheduling, or production device having a scale that allows it to be used directly within the flow of products in a product family, so that operations no longer require unnecessary transport and waiting. Contrast with **monument**. Current recommended practice says that machines should be no more than three times larger than the part they are intended to produce.

robotics: the field of computer science and engineering concerned with creating robots—devices that can move and respond to sensory input. Robots are used in factories to perform high-precision jobs such as welding and riveting. They are also used in special situations that would be dangerous for humans—for example, in cleaning toxic wastes or defusing bombs. See **computer-aided manufacturing**.

robust design: when a procedure or process is not sensitive to variations from its inputs or to deviations from its underlying assumptions, it has a robust design. Setting the process targets using the process interactions increase the likelihood of the design being robust. Also called *robustness*.

root cause: The "first" or most basic cause of a problem, often hidden by more secondary or superficial causes, which, when fixed, don't solve the fundamental or core problem. See **cause**. See also **five whys**.

run chart: a simple monitoring tool that indicates a trend over a specified time. Observed data is plotted in sequence and connected by a line to show runs. These charts can be used to monitor variations from average, increasing or decreasing performance, or any other change in normal data patterns. See **business process tools** for links to other tools.

runner: See **materials handler**.

S

safety stock: finished goods available within the value steam to meet takt time due to *internal constraints or inefficiencies*. Also called *safety inventory*. Contrast with **buffer stock**. The reduction of buffer and safety stock is always a target of continuous improvement.

scatter diagram: uses data points to plot a pattern that shows the relationship or correlation between pairs of variables or factors. This tool is extremely useful to detect the cause of a problem, the strength of a relationship, and how the change of one variable can affect another. See **business process tools** for links to other tools.

scheduling box: See **heijunka box**.

scientific method: the best way yet discovered to winnow the truth from delusion. Briefly, the process is: (1) Observe some aspect of the world. (2) Invent a hypothesis (a tentative description) consistent with what has been observed. (3) Use the hypothesis to make predictions. (4) Test those predictions with experiments or further observations and modify the hypothesis in the light of the results. (5) Repeat steps 3 and 4 until there are no discrepancies between theory and experiment and/or observation. When consistency is obtained the hypothesis becomes a *theory*—a coherent set of propositions that explains a class of phenomena. The theory then becomes a framework with which to explain observations and make predictions. (Description of scientific method from Jose Wudka, University of California.) See **DNA of Toyota** for how these principles are applied to manufacturing.

second-look value engineering: the application of value engineering principles during the last part of the planning stage and the first part of the development and product preparation stage to improve the value and function of existing *components*. Contrast with **zero-look** and **first-look value engineering**. See also **value engineering**.

second-tier supplier: a firm that supplies a first-tier supplier. See **first-tier supplier** and **third-tier supplier**. These terms basically indicate how far away in the supply chain a supplier is from the final assembly or product. They are also a matter of perspective. For example, Company B's first tier supplier may be company A's second tier supplier, etc.

SEDAC: See **system for enhancing daily activities through creativity**.

seiso, seiton, seiri, and seiketsu: four of the five Japanese terms for five S. (**Shitsuke** is the other.) See **five S**.

sensei: Japanese term for a "personal teacher" with mastery of a body of knowledge.

sequence: a metric that is used in the **build-to-schedule** formula to determine how well customer product specifications are being met. Sequence is the number of units built on a given day in the scheduled order (which means only the units after the first unit that have a sequence number larger than all their predecessors). Sequence is calculated by dividing the actual units built to sequence by the actual units built to **mix**.

set in order: the second activity in 5S. It involves identifying the best location for each item kept in an area and using **location indicators** to show placement and set height and size limits for storage. This activity is sometimes referred to as *stabilize*. See **five S**.

setup: See **changeover**.

seven deadly wastes: See **seven muda**.

seven muda: Taiichi Ohno's original categories of the non-value-adding wastes found in physical production. His seven wastes are *overproduction* (in excess of demand), *waiting* (for the next processing step), unnecessary *transport* of materials (for example, between process villages or facilities), *overprocessing* of parts (due to poor tool and product design), *excess inventory* (more than the absolute minimum needed), unnecessary *movement* (unnecessary reaching or walking, or looking for parts, tools, prints, information, etc.), and the production of *defective parts* (or spoilage). See also **waste**.

Shewhart cycle: See **plan-do-check-act cycle**.

shine: the third activity in 5S. It involves cleaning everything thoroughly, adopting cleaning as a continuous form of inspection, and coming up with innovative ways to keep dirt, grime, and other contaminants from accumulating. See **five S**.

Shingo, Shigeo: Japanese industrial engineer known for his skill in improving manufacturing processes, he helped revolutionize the way we manufacture goods. Shingo's paramount quality contribution was his development in the 1960s of **poka-yoke** and **source inspection** systems, which emphasized the practical achievement of **zero defects** by good engineering and process investigation. The **Shingo Prize** for Excellence in Manufacturing, considered the "Noble Prize" of manufacturing, was named in honor of him. Shingo authored numerous books that have been translated into English and are available through Productivity Press, Portland, Oregon. See **five whys** and **single-minute exchange of die**.

Shingo Prize: an award "for excellence in manufacturing," administered by the Utah State University College of Business in partnership with the National Association of Manufacturers. The prize is awarded yearly to North American Companies who can furnish proof of manufacturing improvements. These improvements can be accomplished by focusing their processes according to the "Shingo Prize" model. See **Shingo, Shigeo**.

shitsuke: one of the 5S. See **five S**.

sigma: the Greek letter often used to describe the standard deviation of data. Sigma measures how much a process varies from perfection based on the number of defects per million units. See **six sigma**.

signal kanban: See **kanban**.

signboard: the English translation of the Japanese word "kanban." See **kanban**.

silos: in total quality management language, silos are vertically organized functional departments (self-contained like grain storage towers) that are to be avoided in the lean enterprise. Lean organizations use multidisciplinary teams to break through the walls of these "silos" when designing, making, and delivering products and services to the customer. See **cross-functional management**.

simultaneous changeover: a changeover procedure in which all machines are changed over simultaneously, requiring the line to be completely shut down during the changeover operations. Contrast with **successive changeover**. See also **changeover**.

simultaneous engineering: See **concurrent engineering**.

single-minute exchange of die (SMED): a series of operator techniques pioneered by Shigeo Shingo that result in changeovers of production machinery in *less than ten minutes*. The long-term objective is always zero setup, in which changeovers are instantaneous and do not interfere in any way with one-piece flow. Compare to **one-touch exchange of die** and **zero changeover**. See also **changeover**.

single-piece flow: See **one-piece flow**.

single-point lesson: See **one-point lesson**.

six big losses: major categories of production losses that result from inadequate equipment conditions, which are (1) failure and breakdown loss, (2) setup and adjustment loss, (3) idling and minor stoppage loss, (4) speed loss, (5) quality defect and rework loss, and (6) startup and yield loss. Other ways to categorize production losses are **availability**, **performance**, and **quality losses**. These losses are addressed through **total productive maintenance**.

six sigma: the concept/philosophy/slogan originally coined by Motorola and a methodology that provides tools for improving business processes. Six sigma aims at a defect rate of no more than 3.4 defects per million chances. The increase in performance and decrease in process variation due to this methodology results in high quality product, better employee morale, and large improvements in profit. In practice, six sigma incorporates a statistical point of view and a toolkit with a leaders-developing-leaders approach to implementation in the form of the **black belt** certification process.

SKU: See **stock-keeping unit**.

small-lot production: the manufacture (ideally) of one unit at a time, with the smallest number of goods being produced, allowing for leveled production. Contrast with **large-lot production**.

SMED: See **single-minute exchange of die**.

soft data: subjective, qualitative information based on personal perceptions, opinions, judgments, and feelings. Contrast with **hard data**.

SOP: See **standard operating procedure**.

sort: the first activity in 5S. It involves sorting through all items in an area—tools, parts, instructions, etc.—and placing **red tags** on items that do not belong and moving them to a temporary holding area. The items in the holding area are then relocated, sold, or given away by a predetermined time. See **five S**.

source inspection: inspection performed at the point(s) at which a product is made to find errors. Once errors have been detected at their source, measures can be taken to try to prevent them. *Vertical* source inspection traces problems back through the process flow to identify and control external conditions that affect quality. *Horizontal* source inspection identifies and controls the conditions within an operation that affect quality. See **inspection**.

spaghetti chart: a map of the path taken by a specific product as it moves along the value stream in a mass-production organization. The product's route typically looks like a plate of spaghetti.

SPC: See **statistical process control**.

special cause: a cause that is *sporadic*, unusual, and *correctable*. Contrast with **common cause**. See **con-**

trol chart and **statistical process control** for further discussion.

specialization of labor: See **division of labor**.

sporadic loss: the gap between actual equipment effectiveness and its optimal potential when a loss increases suddenly *beyond its usual range.* Sporadic losses are due to incidents. These may be sudden changes in process conditions. The solution is to regain the original or standard situation. Contrast with **chronic loss**. See **statistical process control**.

stakeholders: persons, groups, or institutions that have an interest in the organization's survival and success. These people are significantly impacted by and can influence the organization. Stakeholders include owners, stockholders, managers, employees, customers or users, competitors, suppliers, and the external community. Also called *constituents.* The term can also be used to mean people who are affected by and can influence a *project* but who are not directly involved with doing the project work.

standard costing: a management accounting system that allocates costs to products based on the *machine hours and labor hours available* to produce them during a given period of time. This cost system encourages managers to make unneeded products or the wrong mix of products to minimize cost-per-product by fully utilizing machines and labor. Contrast with **target costing** and **activity-based costing**.

standard operating procedure (SOP): instructions that cover operations. The scope may be extensive. These instructions may involve regulations, standards, and specifications, and take the form of manuals, change notices, and electronic communications.

standard work: an agreed upon set of work procedures that effectively combines people, materials, and machines to maintain quality, efficiency, safety, and predictability. Work is described precisely in terms of cycle time, work in process, sequence, takt time, layout, and the inventory needed to conduct the activity. Standard work begins as an improvement baseline and evolves into a **reliable method**. It establishes the best activities and sequence steps to maximize performance and minimize waste.

standard work combination sheet (SWCS): a form used in cellular manufacturing to show the cumulative operating time of a process. It combines elements of the **process capacity table** and the **time observation sheet** with the addition of **takt time**.

standard work sheet (SWS): a form used in cellular manufacturing that combines product routing and **process mapping** to depict the activity being analyzed in terms of operator tasks, material, and machines used in a specified production sequence. After iterative improvements, this form will become the basis for standard work in that work activity.

standardization: to promote conformity by means of uniform criteria and practices. As applied to management, see **policy deployment**. As applied to manufacturing processes, see **standard work**.

standardize: the fourth activity in 5S. It involves creating the rules (standards) for maintaining and controlling the conditions that have been established after implementing the first three Ss. See **five S**.

standards: rules or examples that provide clear expectations. They can be based upon authority, consensus arising from experience, data collection, benchmarking, and/or testing. Standards established by a respected authority or by consensus evolve with time. Those based on the summary results of science and commercialization also change, but less frequently. Some standards are significant technical specifications that remain constant.

standby time: a form of waste in which the operator has to monitor the operations of a machine or wait for another operator to complete his or her work. See **seven muda** and **waste**.

statistical process control (SPC): a system of statistical techniques that uses control charts to capture problem data by focusing on one or more critical factors in the manufacturing process and using the data to determine when to stop a faulty process. It involves an understanding of *variation* and the distinction between common (chronic) and special (sporadic) causes. When a process is "in control," variation is consistent over time. A process is out of control when special causes exist. Statistical process control concentrates on the *tools* associated with a process.

See **control chart, chronic loss, sporadic loss**, and **statistical quality control**.

statistical quality control (SQC): the application of statistical techniques to control product quality. The focus is the *end product* whereas **statistical process control** focuses on the *tools used in the process*.

stock turns: an inventory measure of how frequently the stock, raw material, work-in-process, and finished goods are turned over in relation to the sales of a product.

stock-keeping unit (SKU): an inventory identification number that can identify a single product by style, size, color, etc., or even more detailed differentiation such as serial number. Compare to **bar code**.

storyboard: a poster-size visual representation to exhibit the activities of a lean project team and the key information they have discovered. Storyboards serve to inform, educate, and motivate other workers and teams.

strategic intent: a firmly established direction or desired outcome established at the company's strategic level and for strategic reasons.

strategic partnering: a formal or informal relationship between two or more enterprises for their mutual benefit, usually focused on enriching their ability *to penetrate a market or to service existing or new value streams*. This relationship may have a defined duration. Compare with **co-makership**.

strategic planning: planning done at the senior management level where broad directions and initiatives are established to achieve the organization's mission.

strategy: the steps/means to achieve the desired outcome of the strategic plan that informs and shapes **policy deployment** activities.

strategy management: See **policy management**.

strength: the capacity or demonstrated ability for achieving a desired result or creating a desired effect. In an organization, a strength is often referred to as a **core competency**. Contrast with **weakness**.

structure: the arrangement, organization, and interrelation of people and information in support of business operations.

successive changeover: a changeover method in which each machine is changed over as soon as its current step is no longer needed, occurring while other parts of the line are still in production and thereby eliminating the need to shut down during changeover operations. Contrast with **simultaneous changeover**. See also **changeover**.

suggestion system: a practice often employed by organizations to provide a conduit for all personnel to contribute ideas for the focused or general improvement of all areas of the company. These systems can be structured to emphasize individual suggestions, team suggestions, or both. To develop a system that will return benefit, the company needs to promote and reward employee participation as well as provide and encourage employee education. Two important aspects of suggestion systems that are often overlooked are (1) the need to carefully and thoroughly design and manage them and (2) the need to provide feedback to employees about whether and how their suggestions are being implemented. The lack of these two factors often leads to the failure of suggestion systems.

supermarket: storage of a set amount of finished goods or work-in-process within the value stream to allow for a pull system when pure continuous flow is not possible. Material can be removed from the supermarket and replaced only with a **kanban card**.

supplier kanban: See **kanban**.

supply chain: *all suppliers* involved in the *manufacture* of any single component used in a particular end product, beginning with the manufacturer of the simplest component and ending with the manufacturer of the end product. Compare to **customer/supplier chain** and **value chain**.

survival triplet: the three related product characteristics of price, quality, and functionality that can make or break a product. When these are well-managed a product is said to be within its **survival zone**.

survival zone: the area between the minimums and maximums of price, quality, and functionality (the

survival triplet) that a product must stay within to be successful.

sustain: the fifth activity of 5S. At this step, persons and teams ensure adherence to standards through ongoing communication, training, and, very importantly, self-discipline. When thoroughly implemented, sustain will include the use of **visual displays**, **visual metrics**, and **visual controls**. See **five S**.

SWCS: See **standard work combination sheet**.

synergy: the combination of two or more people, elements, factors, or units, to achieve an effect of which neither is individually capable and which results in more than the sum of the two or more parts.

system: a set or an arrangement of things so closely related or connected as to form a unit or organic whole. From **system dynamics** we learn that systems have typical "behavior" patterns and feedback loops that are both positive and negative. Typical patterns of complex systems include resistance, drift to low performance, general parameter insensitivity, heightened sensitivity to particular influence points, and conflict between long-term and short-term response. Systems also exhibit patterns of growth, decline, oscillation, equilibrium-seeking, and goal-seeking.

system dynamics: a *methodology* for studying and managing complex feedback systems, such as those found in business and other social systems. Modifying the link between any two factors independently cannot predict how the whole system will respond. Only the study of the *whole system as a feedback system* will lead to correct understanding and action. Often, the first problem identified is found to be a symptom of a still greater problem.

System dynamics identifies a problem, develops a hypothesis, *builds a computer model* of the system at the root of the problem, tests the constructed model for validity, and then tests solutions to the problem by *making changes in the model*. The field developed initially from the work of Jay W. Forrester and his seminal book *Industrial Dynamics* (1961). Since then, applications have grown to include public management and policy, biological and medical modeling, energy and the environment, etc. See **cybernetics**, **systems theory**, and **systems thinking**.

system for enhancing daily activities through creativity (SEDAC): In *Building Organizational Fitness: Management Methodology for Transformation and Strategic Advantage* (Productivity Press), Dr. Ryuji Fukuda expanded CEDAC into a comprehensive strategic improvement process. He named this new process SEDAC (system for enhancing daily activities through creativity). This process goes beyond problem solving to include the continuous, systematic improvement of all aspects of a business. It includes the use of a modified **Johari's window** and a **policy and objectives** (x-type) **matrix**. See **cause and effect diagram with the addition of cards (CEDAC)**.

systems theory: in 1940, biologist Ludwig von Bertalanffy, reacting against reductionism, emphasized that real systems are open to, and interact with, their environments, and that they can aquire *qualitatively new properties through emergence*, resulting in continual evolution. Instead of reducing an entity (for example, the human body) to properties of its parts or elements (organs or cells), systems theory focuses on the arrangement of and relations of the parts, which make up *a whole that is independent of the concrete substance of the elements* (whether particles, cells, transistors, people, etc.). Systems concepts include system-environment boundries, input, output, process, state, heirarchy, goal-directedness, and information. See **cybernetics**, **system dynamics**, and **systems thinking**.

systems thinking: whereas traditional analysis focuses on breaking the whole of what is being studied into constituent parts to scrutinize those parts, systems thinking focuses on how the thing being studied interacts with the other constituents of the system of which it is a part—how the elements interact to produce behavior. So, as any issue is being studied, instead of focusing on smaller and smaller aparts of the system under study, systems thinking expands its view to take into account larger and larger numbers of interactions. This sometimes results in strikingly different conclusions than those generated by traditional forms of analysis, especially when what is being studied is dynamically complex or has a great deal of feedback from other sources, internal or external.

Systems thinking looks at the same kinds of systems from the same perspectives as does **system**

dynamics. It also constructs causal-loop diagrams. But it rarely takes the additional steps of constructing and testing a computer model and testing alternative policies in the model. See also **cybernetics** and **systems theory**.

T

Taguchi methods: originally developed by Genichi Taguchi for the purpose of simplifying quality control procedures in Japan. His methods are basically a form of experimental design to achieve near optimal quality characteristics (reduce variability) for processes and products. Numerous experimental design procedures, based on his methods, have since been adapted or developed to achieve this objective.

takt image: the vision of the ideal state in which you have eliminated waste and improved the performance of the value stream to where it is possible to achieve one-piece flow based on takt time.

takt time: the rate at which product must be turned out to satisfy market demand. It is determined by dividing the available production time by the rate of **customer demand**. For example, if customers demand 240 widgets per day and the factory operates 480 minutes per day, takt time is two minutes. If customers want two new products designed per month, takt time is two weeks. It is a *calculated number*, not a reflection of your capability. It sets the pace of production to match the rate of customer demand.

target cost: the cost of developing and producing a product that must not be exceeded in order for the customer to be satisfied with the value of the product and the manufacturer to be satisfied with return on investment. The target cost is set after subtracting a product's target profit margin from its target selling price (**allowable cost**). A target cost will be set, which may or may not be different than the allowable cost. This cost target becomes the cost-reduction challenge. See **draft target cost** and **final target cost**.

target cost management: the systematic process of planning and delivering products and services by determining their sales prices, establishing a continuously adjusting set of downward-ratcheting, highly challenging target costs, and motivating employees to be vigilant about cost reduction opportunities. In this way quality and functionally of products and services will give value to the customer as well as profit to the company.

target costing: a strategic cost-management process for reducing the total costs of products, services, and capital equipment *at the planning and design stages*. It concentrates on integrating the efforts of all relevant departments such as marketing, engineering, production, and accounting, as well as related suppliers. Target costs are set, on the one hand, with price points for products and capital equipment that respect the customer's perception of value and, on the other hand, that meet the company's required return on investment. Target revenues and profits, as well as costs, are expressed in terms of a profit plan. In the design and planning stages, target costs are achieved through **value engineering** and other techniques. In the production stage, target costs are achieved through **kaizen costing**, which relies heavily upon employee involvement. Target costing is sometimes referred to as **profit management**. See also **chained target costing**.

target costing chain: two or more target costing systems whose pricing abilities have become interlinked. The first link in the chain is the firm that *can't set prices for its buyer* but can set prices for the firm it is supplied by. The last link in the chain is the firm that *can't set prices for the firm it is supplied by* but whose prices have nevertheless been set by its *buyer*. See also **chained target costing**.

target-means diagram: the visual representation of the relationship between an initiative's *targets* and the *means* that will achieve them.

target statement: as applied to problem solving and process improvement or as used on a CEDAC chart, a good target statement should quantify a target, specify the target date, and specify the measure. It should be short and focused. A good example is: "By *xx*, defects on line A will be reduced to 3 or less, as measured by each shift (not average per shift but actual per shift)." See **problem statement**.

team: a group of people who rely on cooperation, trust, and communication to achieve a common set of objectives or targets. A **cross-functional team** is made up of people from different departments in an organization. A **tiger team** is put together to get quick results. Many factors combine to make groups effective or ineffective-team composition, leadership, interpersonal skills, clear charter, reliable methods, personal commitment, etc. See **team charter** and **team stages**.

team charter: a document that includes but is not limited to (1) a clear definition of the team's mission, (2) a statement of each team member's roles and responsibilities, (3) a description of the scope of the team's responsibility and authority, (4) the project deadlines, (5) a list of metrics or targets, and (6) a list of deliverables (outcomes).

team stages: natural and expected phases that a group of people will go through to achieve an effective working relationship. Psychologist B.W. Tuckman called these stages forming, storming, norming, and performing. At the *forming* stage team members test the new situation and choose roles. In the *storming* stage members resolve how to deal with the conflicts that will inevitably arise. In the *norming* stage group members agree on group behaviors and develop a sense of group cohesiveness. In the *performing* stage group output is high. We could add a *transforming* stage, in which the group members have become very effective **change agents** beyond the boundaries of the group.

teardown analysis: the analysis of competitive products in terms of basic materials, parts, and manufacturing methods.

technology: the entire body of methods, processes, hardware, software, and materials used to achieve commercial or industrial objectives. Also, broadly speaking, the ways that a social group provides itself with the material objects of its civilization. For example, the **division of labor**, a method for organizing work, was the foundation technology of the **industrial revolution**. Later, Watt's steam engine was harnessed to amplify the productivity inherent in the division of labor. The *reintegration of labor*, another method for organizing work, is the principal technology of lean production.

technology deployment: See **quality function deployment**.

TEI: total employee involvement. See **employee involvement**.

theory of constraints: Eliyahu Goldratt's theory that every company has constraints or it would be making infinite profit. Therefore he has developed a five-step process of improvement with the objective of eliminating or reducing constraints. The steps are (1) identify the constraint, (2) decide how to exploit the constraint, (3) subordinate all other resources to solving the restraint, (4) elevate the constraint, and (5) if the constraint has been solved, return to step 1. See **constraint**.

therblig: the name for an elemental movement used in time motion studies. Contractor F.B. Gilbreth coined this term and identified eighteen basic movements. (The term is Gilbreth spelled backwards, except for the "th".) Saving wasted motion is one way to eliminate waste. See **seven muda** and **waste**.

third-tier supplier: a firm that supplies a second-tier supplier. See **second-tier supplier** and **first-tier supplier**. These terms essentially indicate how far away in the supply chain a supplier is from the final assembly or product. They are also a matter of perspective. For example, Company B's first tier supplier may be company A's second tier supplier, etc.

throughput time: the rate at which sold production work proceeds through a *manufacturing process*. This includes both processing time and waiting time. Compare and contrast with **lead time, manufacturing lead time**, and **processing time**.

tiger marks: alternating black and yellow stripes that draw attention to a safety hazard. When these stripes are on marking tape, the tape is called *tiger tape*. A **five S for safety** technique.

tiger team: a group of people who are assigned the task of generating the best implemented set of improvements in a relatively short period of time. See **team**.

time observation sheet (TOS): a form used in cellular manufacturing to document and analyze an operation with the goal of removing waste. The sequence and time is noted for each task, as well as whether the task is value-adding, non-value-adding, or a non-cyclic task. Some of the calculations obtained from the time observation sheet will be used in the **process capacity table**. See **standard work combination sheet**.

top-down management: See **authoritarian management**.

total cycle time (TCT): as an overall measure, this is the length of time between when material for a product enters a plant and the point at which the finished product is shipped. It is the total of the cycle times for each individual operation or cell in a value stream and refers to the actual production capability of a plant. Cycle time improvements focus on analyzing operations and eliminating bottlenecks. If cycle time from a *complete* process can be reduced to equal **takt time**, product can be made in **one-piece flow**. See **cycle time**.

total employee involvement (TEI): See **employee involvement**.

total productive maintenance (TPM): a company-wide approach and a series of methods, originally pioneered by Nippondenso (a member firm of the Toyota group), to enlist operators in the design, selection, correction, and maintenance of equipment to ensure that every machine or process is always able to perform its required tasks without interrupting or slowing down defect-free production. Total productive maintenance includes **autonomous maintenance, early equipment management, focused equipment improvement, predictive maintenance, and preventive maintenance**. The principal performance measure of TPM is **overall equipment effectiveness**.

total productivity management (TP management): a
management approach that organizes and prioritizes
the activities of customer-oriented product manufacturing by coordinating objectives coming from the
top down with proposals and strategies emerging
from the bottom up. These objectives and strategies
are expressed in visible form with the total productivity (TP) deployment diagram.

total quality management (TQM): an approach
advanced in Japan by Dr. W. Edwards Deming.
The premise of this approach is that *all* operations
have a quality aspect that can be perfected. True
quality can only be achieved through constant
measurement and monitoring and it requires a continuous, cohesive effort by every person in the company. TQM can be applied to advantage in any
area: education, business, patient care, government,
etc. Also called *total quality control (TQC)*. See
Deming, W. Edwards.

Toyota Production System (TPS): a manufacturing
efficiency model built upon three key factors:
reduced lot sizes to allow for production flexibility,
the control of production parts so that parts are
always available when and where they are needed,
and the arrangement of production equipment in
logical order of assembly. See **Ohno, Taiichi**. See
also **DNA of Toyota**.

TPM: See **total productive maintenance**.

TP management: See **total productivity
management**.

TPM tag: a two-part tag used during the initial stages of total productive maintenance to label the parts of the equipment that need to be repaired or restored. The two parts of the tag involve the original, which stays with the item tagged, and a copy, which is removed and used to track action and resolution.

TPS: See **Toyota Production System**.

TQM: See **total quality management**.

transport kanban: Also called *move kanban*. See **kanban**.

triangle kanban: a special kind of production kanban with a triangle shape that signals when the **reorder point** is reached in the **kanban system**.

triangulation: in any conflict situation, this interpersonal phenomena occurs when an individual or group goes to a third party to talk about the conflict rather than dealing with the individual or group with whom the conflict exists. A dysfunctional pattern that defeats cooperation and teamwork.

turn-back analysis: an examination of the flow of a product through a set of production operations to see how often the product has to be sent backwards for rework or scrap.

type 1 error: rejecting the null hypothesis when it is true; that is, a relationship between two variables is assumed to exist when none actually does exist. (The null hypothesis states that there is no relationship between two variables or no difference between two groups.)

type 2 error: accepting the null hypothesis when it is false; that is, a relationship between two variables is assumed not to exist when one actually does exist. (The null hypothesis states that there is no relationship between two variables or no difference between two groups.)

U

U-shaped cell: a cell in the shape of a letter 'U" that enables one or more operators to produce and transfer parts one piece or one small lot at a time. It also creates a layout where the location for the input of material is very close to the output location. See **cell** and **cell layout**.

uptime: the capacity to produce and provide goods and services. Sometimes used to refer to the revenue producing operation of a machine.

V

VA: See **value analysis**.

value: when a product or service has been perceived or appraised to fulfill a need or desire—*as defined by the customer*—the product or service may be said to have value or worth. Components of value may include quality, utility, functionality, capacity, aesthetics, timeliness or availability, price, etc.

value-added ratio (VAR): one of the central metrics for the lean enterprise that represents the percentage of **manufacturing lead time** actually spent doing **value-adding** activities. The value-added ratio is determined by dividing total value-added time of a process by the manufacturing lead time of that process *x* 100.

value-adding: the creation of value through waste-free operations and processes. Any operation or activity that changes, converts, or transforms material into a product or service the customer is willing to pay for. Contrast with **non-value-adding**.

value-adding management (VAM): the management process of the lean, cross-functional organization that utilizes policy management to integrate employee-involvement methods such as total quality management, just-in-time, total productive maintenance, and concurrent engineering in order to consistently achieve customer-focused business objectives.

value analysis (VA): the very detailed analytical process of evaluating a sequence of operations as to the value each operation adds at each particular stage. It is part of **value engineering**. See **business process tools** for links to other tools.

value chain: the entire chain of *value creation* from materials to production to final consumption, involving *multiple companies*. A value chain is a **supply chain** plus the *final* customers. Compare to **customer/supplier chain**.

value engineering (VE): the systematic, interdisciplinary approach that assesses all operations as to the value they provide to the *operational* portion of the value stream on a movement by movement basis. See **zero-look, first-look**, and **second-look value engineering**.

value stream: all the activities (both value-added and non-value added) required within one company to design and provide a specific product from its conception to launch, from order to delivery, and from raw materials into the hands of the customer.

value stream management: a way to plan and link lean initiatives throughout the value stream by systematic data analysis. It is a several-step process using lean concepts and tools from the Toyota Production System to minimize the waste that prevents a smooth, continuous flow of product along the value stream.

value stream mapping: the identification of all the specific activities (material *and* information flow) occurring along the value stream for a particular product or product family, usually represented pictorially in a value stream map. Also called *value stream process mapping*.

VAM: See **value-adding management**.

VAR: See **value-added ratio**.

variance analysis: the analysis of causes for the difference between what is actual and some other norm such as what was expected, budgeted, projected, estimated, etc. See **business process tools** for links to other tools.

variety reduction: a standardization initiative that attempts to eliminate nonfunctional differences from model-to-model and part to part so as to increase the efficiency of the production operation.

VE: See **value engineering**.

vertical coordination: in a supplier chain, the processes operating among firms in *different tiers* to maintain the value of the whole network. Contrast with **horizontal coordination**. See also **first tier, second-tier**, and **third tier supplier**.

visible waste: the *tangible, physical waste* such as in-process inventory and defects that can be seen at the worksite. Contrast with **invisible waste**. See also **seven muda** and **waste**.

vision: a positive and inspiring idea about how and why the business serves its customers. The vision should be initiated by the leadership but must be shared and supported by everyone in the organization. Some good examples of brief vision statements are (1) "We love to fly and it shows"—Delta, (2) "The tightest ship in the shipping business"—UPS, (3) "We bring good things to light"—GE. A vision should be supported by a comprehensive **mission statement**.

visual control: as originally coined, this meant the control of the workplace by the *visual* regulation of operations, performance goals, tool and parts placement, etc., so that a production process or other system could be understood at a glance. However, visual controls can appeal to any or all of the five senses. In a library for the blind, they might be tactile or audible. In the broadest sense, visual control refers to just-in-time information that ensures the fast and proper execution of operations and processes. Some **mistake-proofing devices** may be classified as visual controls. See **levels of visual control**.

visual control system: an integrated set of visual controls designed to create a transparent and waste-free environment. For example, the interstate highway system uses an elaborate visual control system to ensure the safe and smooth flow of high-speed traffic.

visual display: the use of easily seen and easily understood information to control the environment and its activities. Displays may include **location indicators**, signboards, status boards, **one-point lessons**, checklists, worksheets, diagrams, area maps, etc. Displays may pertain to equipment use, operations, processes, metrics, storage, safety, quality, movement in an area, or general use of the environment.

visual factory: the application of **visual control** and a **visual management system** *on the shop floor.* On a visually controlled shop floor, anyone in the area should have a good idea about the who, what, where, when, why, and how of activities and equipment within minutes or seconds.

visual management system: systematic attention to the goal of *companywide integration* of visual operation, including workplace organization and standardization (the **five S**), **visual display**, **visual metrics**, and **visual control**.

visual metrics: the display of measurements important to maintaining and improving operations and processes so that everyone involved can easily view and comprehend them. See **lean measurables** and **manufacturing measurables**.

visual office: the application of **visual control** and a **visual management system** *in the administrative and support areas* of the company. In a visually controlled office, anyone in the area should have a good idea about the who, what, where, when, why, and how of activities and equipment within minutes or seconds.

voice of the customer: the desires and expectations of the customer, which are of primary importance in the development of new products, services, and the daily conduct of the business.

volume: a metric used in the **build-to-schedule** formula to determine how well customer product specifications are being met. Volume is determined by dividing the actual units produced by the units that were scheduled (ordered).

W

waste: basically, anything that adds cost or time without adding value. There are many different kinds of wastes in manufacturing. See **seven muda**.

water beetle or water spider: See **materials handler**.

weakness: lacking the skill, ability, or proficiency to function properly or accomplish goals. An organization's weaknesses put it at risk. Organizational weaknesses are made clear by **gap analysis**. Contrast with **strength**.

window analysis: a modification of **Johari's window**, window analysis is a technique to determine the root cause(s) of a performance problem by analyzing the contribution of any two parties (individuals or organizational units) to the problem. Party X and Party Y mark answers to questions about their practices, procedures, and work instructions on a tic-tac-toe-like grid. Practices, procedures, and work instructions have three categories: known and practiced, known and not practiced, or unknown. See **business process tools** for links to other tools.

withdrawal kanban: See **kanban**.

work cell: See **cell**.

work in process: material in the process of having value added to it—being converted into salable goods. In lean manufacturing the quantity of work in process is controlled for maximum efficiency of product flow.

workplace organization and standardization: See **five S**.

workplace scan: the preliminary activity of five S, it is an evaluation of workplace conditions and activities prior to beginning the five steps. Boundaries for the cleanup area and the stakeholders are identified, an area map and arrow diagram is drawn, and "before" conditions are photographed and checked-off on the Workplace Scan Diagnostic Checklist to obtain an improvement baseline. See **five S**.

world class manufacturing: an operational strategy of continuous improvement powered by the synergy of total quality management, just-in-time, total employee involvement, and total productive maintenance. These processes promote the production of quality goods at a minimum cost, meeting or exceeding customer expectations, and thereby enabling the organization to compete effectively in *world markets*.

world-wide web: internet system for hypertext linking of multimedia documents, allowing users to move from one Internet site to another and to inspect the information that is available without using complicated commands and protocols.

X, Y, Z

X-type matrix: See **matrix diagram**.

yellow belt: sometimes used to refer to a person who has a basic knowledge of six sigma but who does not implement improvement projects or lead improvement teams on their own as does a **green belt** or **black belt**.

zero changeover: A changeover procedure performed in less than three minutes or within one production cycle, often, but not necessarily, with automated changeover equipment. Zero changeover is especially important for suppliers to customers who practice just-in-time. Compare to **one-touch exchange of die** and **single-minute exchange of die**.

zero defects: the concept introduced by Philip Crosby, when he was a quality manager at Martin Marietta, of manufacturing products that have no (*zero*) defects. See **mistake-proofing**.

zero-look value engineering: the application of value engineering principles at the earliest stage—the concept proposal stage—of the design process in order to introduce *forms of functionality* that have not previously existed. Contrast with **first-look** and **second-look value engineering**. See also **value engineering**.

zero quality control (ZQC): a comprehensive system of quality management that incorporates (1) self-inspection of quality by operators, (2) successive inspection of incoming quality by operator, and (3) the systematic use of mistake-proofing devices to control quality at the source. Compare to **six sigma**.

Bibliography

Akao, Yoji, editor. *Quality Function Deployment: Integrating Customer Requirements into Product Design.* Portland, Oregon: Productivity Press, 1990.

Ammerman, Max. *The Root Cause Analysis Handbook: A Simplified Approach to Identifying, Correcting, and Reporting Workplace Errors.* Portland, Oregon: Productivity Press, 1998.

Barrett, Derm. *Fast Focus on TQM: A Concise Guide to Companywide Learning.* Portland, Oregon: Productivity Press, 1994.

Blank, Ronald. *The Basics of Quality Auditing.* Portland, Oregon: Productivity Press, 1999.

Breyfogle III, Forrest W. Implementing *Six Sigma: Smarter Solutions Using Statistical Methods.* New York: John Wiley and Sons, Inc., 1999.

Campbell, John Dixon. *Uptime: Strategies for Excellence in Management.* Portland, Oregon: Productivity Press, 1995.

Christopher, William F., and Carl G. Thor. *Handbook for Productivity Measurement and Improvement.* Portland, Oregon: Productivity Press, 1993.

Cooper, Robin, and Regine Slagmulder. *Supply Chain Development for the Lean Enterprise: Interorganizational Cost Management.* Portland, Oregon: Productivity Press; Montvale, New Jersey:

The IMA Foundation for Applied Research, Inc., 1999.

———. *Target Costing and Value Engineering.* Portland, Oregon: Productivity Press; Montvale, New Jersey: The IMA Foundation for Applied Research, Inc., 1997.

Edelson, Norman M., and Carole L. Bennett. *Process Discipline: How to Maximize Profitability through Manufacturing Consistency.* Portland, Oregon: Productivity Press, 1998.

Fukuda, Ryuji. *Building Organizational Fitness: Management Methodology for Transformation and Strategic Advantage.* Portland, Oregon: Productivity Press, 1997.

———. *CEDAC: A Tool for Continuous Systematic Improvement.* Portland, Oregon: Productivity Press, 1989.

Goldratt, Eliyahu M., and Jeff Cox. *The Goal: A Process of Ongoing Improvement (2nd revised edition).* Great Barrington, Massachusetts: North River Press, 1992.

Gross, Clifford M. *The Right Fit: The Power of Ergonomics as a Competitive Strategy.* Portland, Oregon: Productivity Press, 1996.

Hirano, Hiroyuki. *5S for Operators: 5 Pillars of the Visual Workplace.* Portland, Oregon: Productivity Press, 1996.

Jackson, Thomas L. *Corporate Diagnosis: Setting the Global Standard for Excellence. Constance Dyer, contributor.* Portland, Oregon: Productivity Press, 1996.

——. *Implementing a Lean Management System.* Karen R. Jones, contributor. Portland, Oregon: Productivity Press, 1996.

Japan Institute of Plant Maintenance, editor. *Focused Equipment Improvement for TPM Teams (ShopFloor Series).* Portland, Oregon: Productivity Press, 1991.

Kaplan, Robert S. and Robin Cooper. *Cost and Effect: Using Integrated Cost Systems to Drive Profitability and Performance.* Boston: Harvard Business School Press, 1997.

Lewis, C. Patrick. *Building a Shared Vision: A Leader's Guide to Aligning the Organization.* Portland, Oregon: Productivity Press, 1997.

Liker, Jeffrey K., editor. *Becoming Lean: Inside Story of U.S. Manufacturers.* Portland, Oregon: Productivity Press, 1998.

Michalski, Walter. *Tool Navigator: The Master Guide for Teams.* Diana G. King, contributor. Portland Oregon: Productivity Press, 1997.

Mikel, Harry, and Richard Schroeder. *Six Sigma: The Breakthrough Management Strategy Revolutionizing the World's Top Corporations.* New York: Doubleday (Currency), 2000.

Monden, Yasuhiro. Cost Reduction Systems: *Target Costing and Kaizen Costing*. Portland, Oregon: Productivity Press, 1995.

Ohno, Taiichi. *Toyota Production System: Beyond Large-Scale Production*. Portland, Oregon: Productivity Press, 1988.

Productivity Development Team. *Autonomous Maintenance Shopfloor TPM Implementation (Participant Guide)*. Portland, Oregon: Productivity Press, 2000.

Productivity Development Team. *5S for Safety Implementation Toolkit (Facilitator Guide)*. Portland, Oregon: Productivity Press, 2000.

Productivity Development Team. *One-Point Lessons: Rapid Transfer of Best Practices for the Shop Floor (Implementation Toolkit Participant Guide)*. Portland, Oregon: Productivity Press, 2000.

Roberts, Nancy, et al. *Introduction to Computer Simulation: A System Dynamics Modeling Approach*. Portland, Oregon: Productivity Press, 1994.

Sekine, Kenichi. *Achieving One-Piece Flow Through Cell Design (Application Workbook)*. Portland, Oregon: Productivity Press, 1992.

Senge, Peter M. *The Fifth Discipline: The Art and Practice of the Learning Organization*. New York: Doubleday Books, 1994.

Shingo, Shigeo. *A Study of the Toyota Production System from an Industrial Engineering Viewpoint (revised edition)*. Portland, Oregon: Productivity Press, 1989.

Stamatis, D.H. *Advanced Quality Planning. A Commonsense Guide to AQP and APQP*. Portland, Oregon: Productivity Press, 1998.

Steinbacher, Herbert R. and Norma L. Steinbacher. *TPM for Amercia. What It Is and Why You Need It*. Portland, Oregon: Productivity Press, 1993.

Suzaki, Kiyoshi. *The New Manufacturing Challenge: Techniques for Continuous Improvement*. New York: The Free Press, 1987.

Tapping, Don. *Value Stream Management: Eight Steps to Planning, Mapping, and Sustaining Lean Improvements (Participant Guide)*. Tom Fabrizio, instructional designer. Portland, Oregon: Productivity Press, 2001.

Tajiri, Masaji, and Fumio Gotoh. *Autonomous Maintenance in Seven Steps: Implementing TPM on the Shop Floor*. Portland Oregon: Productivity Press, 1999.

Womack, James P., and Daniel T. Jones. *Lean Thinking: Banish Waste and Create Wealth in Your Corporation*. New York: Simon and Schuster, 1996.

———. *The Machine That Changed the World: The Story of Lean Production*. Daniel T. Jones and Daniel Roos, contributors. New York: HarperCollins, 1991.

Other materials used to compile this dictionary (listed below) belong to the Productivity Consulting Group and are not for sale. They are given to individuals attending public workshops or in-house company trainings. For information about current trainings, call 1-800-782-0930 or 1-800-615-3387, or visit www.productivityinc.com.

Achieving One-Piece Flow: Implementing Cell Design (Participant Guide).

Achieving Quick Changeover: The SMED System (Participant Guide).

Focused Equipment Improvement (Participant Guide).

Leading World Class Teams: Linking Improvement Strategies to Daily Work (Participant Guide).

Manufacturing Measurables (Participant Guide).

Mistake Proofing: Achieving: Achieving Zero Defects in the Workplace (Participant Guide).

Planning and Implementing Lean Production (Participant Guide).

Planning and Implementing Total Productive Maintenance (Participant Guide).

Pull Production: A Push Toward Lean (Participant Guide).

Understanding and Applying Overall Equipment Effectiveness (Participant Guide).

Value Stream Management: Eight Steps to a Lean Plan (Participant Guide).

Visual Workplace (Participant Guide).

New Titles from Productivity Press

Leading the Lean Initiative: Straight Talk on Cultivating Support and Buy-in

Turn the theories behind lean into a reality. In *Leading the Lean Initiative*, John W. Davis shows you how to lead a lean effort and effectively manage change during your lean transformation. He emphasizes the "human" side of the lean initiative—providing tips for cultivating a culture receptive to change and for gaining employee buy-in. He offers sound advice for manufacturing managers who are trying to lead lean initiatives while dealing with the daily aspects of plant management.

Leading the Lean Initiative is an invaluable resource for any company looking to streamline their processes with lean methodologies and is a must read for managers regardless of their industry.

The Eaton Lean System: An Interactive Introduction to Lean Manufacturing Principles

Bring the basics of lean to the shop floor. Teaming up with the Eaton Corporation, Productivity is proud to bring you a comprehensive introduction to lean—*The Eaton Lean System*. It's a training package with all the features you've been asking for. Integrating the latest in interactivity with informative and powerful video presentations, this innovative software makes the fundamental concepts of lean accessible, interesting and fun!

Seven topic-focused CDs let you tackle lean subjects in the order you choose. You'll get short lessons in each subject before watching examples and completing tasks to clarify the concept. Covering topics such as muda (waste), standardized work, continuous flow, pull systems, kaizen, heijunka (scheduling), and 5S, these CDs enable learners to apply the concepts right away, which makes for a powerful, high-impact learning experience.

To order either of these products or to receive a copy of our full catalog, call us at 1-800-394-6868 or visit our website at www.productivityinc.com.